Microsoft Word Introduction and Certification Study Guide

Microsoft 365 Apps and Office 2019

Daniel John Stine

SDC
PUBLICATIONS

SDC Publications
P.O. Box 1334
Mission, KS 66222
913-262-2664
www.SDCpublications.com
Publisher: Stephen Schroff

ISBN-13: 978-1-63057-371-3
ISBN-10: 1-63057-371-X

Printed and bound in the United States of America.

Foreword

<u>Intended audience</u>

Created for students and professionals, this book teaches the use of Word to create well formatted, high-quality documents. Additionally, anyone interested in practicing for the Microsoft Word (Microsoft 365 Apps and Office 2019) certification exam will also benefit.

<u>Introduction</u>

This book provides a collection of study materials to both learn Word and to prepare for the Microsoft Word (Microsoft 365 Apps and Office 2019) Exam (Exam MO-100). With a range of options for most learning styles, this book will help improve your skill level and provide an additional boost of confidence, which is sure to increase the chances of a successful exam outcome.

Study material for all learning styles, including:

- Printed book
    - o **Introduction to Word** *with no previous experience required*
    - o **Focused Study** *on objective domains*
    - o **Flashcards** *cut out with scissors*
    - o **Exam Day Study Guide** *one page reference*
- Downloads
    - o **Narrated Videos** *with optional captions*
    - o **Practice Software** *Prerequisite: Microsoft Word 365/2019 installed*

The book begins with an overview of the user interface and then dives into the following categories in more detail:

- Manage Documents
- Insert and Format Text, Paragraphs, and Sections
- Manage Tables and Lists
- Create and Manage References
- Insert and Format Graphic Elements
- Manage Document Collaboration

The text concludes with an overview of the included practice exam software download. This software mimics the real exam as much as possible, in terms of user interface, number and types of questions, as well as a time constraint. While this study guide cannot claim to cover every possible question that may arise in the exam, it does help to firm up your basic knowledge to positively deal with most questions… thus, leaving more time to reflect on the more difficult questions.

Two books in one

- Introduction to Word for beginners
  No previous experience is required to use this book to learn Microsoft Word. This book is focused on the basics and building a solid foundation. But, even if you have some experience with Word, the book offers valuable tips and workflows.

- Certification exam study guide
  This book is also geared towards those wishing to formalize the conclusion of their learning experience by taking the Microsoft Word (Microsoft 365 Apps and Office 2019) certification exam.

Errata:
Please check the publisher's website from time to time for any errors or typos found once printed. Simply browse to www.SDCpublications.com, and then navigate to the page for this book. Click the **View/Submit errata** link in the upper right corner of the page. If you find an error, please submit it so we can correct it in the next edition.

You may contact the publisher with comments or suggestions at service@SDCpublications.com.

About the Author:

Daniel John Stine AIA, CSI, CDT, is a registered architect with over twenty years of experience in the field of architecture. He has worked on many multi-million-dollar projects, including a nearly $1 billion dollar hospital project in the Midwest. Throughout these years of professional practice, Stine has leveraged many of the Microsoft Office products to organize and manage complex projects.

He has presented internationally on architecture and design technology in the USA, Canada, Ireland, Scotland, Denmark, Slovenia, Australia and Singapore; and has been a top-rated speaker on several occasions. By invitation, in 2016, he spent a week at Autodesk's largest R&D facility in Shanghai, China, to beta test and brainstorm new features in their flagship architectural design software, Revit.

Committed to furthering the design profession, Stine teaches graduate architecture students at North Dakota State University (NDSU) and has lectured for design programs at NDSU, Northern Iowa State, and University of Minnesota, University of Texas at San Antonio (UTSA) as well as Dunwoody's new School of Architecture in Minneapolis. As an adjunct instructor, Dan previously taught AutoCAD and Revit for twelve years at Lake Superior College. He is a member of the American Institute of Architects (AIA), Construction Specifications Institute (CSI), and Autodesk Developer Network (ADN), Autodesk Expert Elite, and is a Construction Document Technician (issued by CSI).

In addition to Microsoft Office certification study guides, Stine has written multiple books on architectural design software, all written using Microsoft Word, and published by SDC Publications.

You may contact the publisher with comments or suggestions at service@SDCpublications.com.

Many thanks go out to Stephen Schroff and SDC Publications for making this book possible!

Table of Contents

1. Create and Manage Documents

4. Create and Manage References

5. Insert and Format Graphic Elements

6. Manage Document Collaboration

6.0. Collaborating with a team

6.1. Add and manage comments

6.2. Manage change tracking

7. Practice Exam (Provided with this Book)

7.0. Introduction

8. Certification Study Resources

8.1.1 **Exam Day Study Guide**: one page

8.2.1 **Flashcards**: 75 cards

Index

Included Online Resources

Online resources may be download from SDC Publications using access code and instructions on the inside-front cover of this book.

 Practice Exam Software: Test your skills with this included resource

 Videos: 95 short, narrated videos covering each exam outcome

0 Getting Started

0.0 Getting Started

Before you can begin learning the ins and outs of Word, you need to open it up.

0.0.0 Starting Word

Here are the main ways to start Word. Adding the Word icon to the taskbar, at the bottom of the screen, is the most efficient but it is not there by default.

1. Click the **Start Menu**
2. Select **Word** from the list
3. Two additional options:
   a. Type "Word" in the **search**, select Word in the search results list
   b. Most efficient: Right-click on the Word icon in step #2, select "Pin to taskbar," single-click new icon on **taskbar** to start Word.

Starting Word

0.1 User Interface

Word is a powerful and sophisticated program. Because of its powerful feature set, it has a measurable learning curve. However, like anything, when broken down into smaller pieces, we can easily learn to harness the power of Word.

Next, we will walk through the different aspects of the User Interface (UI). As with any program, understanding the user interface, and correct terminology, is the key to using the program's features and using this study guide efficiently.

Home Screen

When Word is first opened, the Home screen is presented, as shown in the image below. Clicking the **Blank workbook** tile (i.e. template) is the quickest way to get working in Word. Use the **Open** option or **Recent/Pinned** files options to access existing Word files. To verify User or Product information use the **Account** command in the lower left. Finally, the **Options** command opens the same-named dialog with a plethora of settings and options to control Word's default behavior.

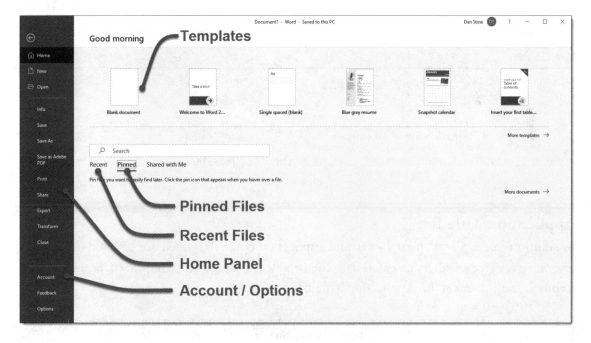

Word Home Screen

The image below highlights important terms to know for the Word user interface.

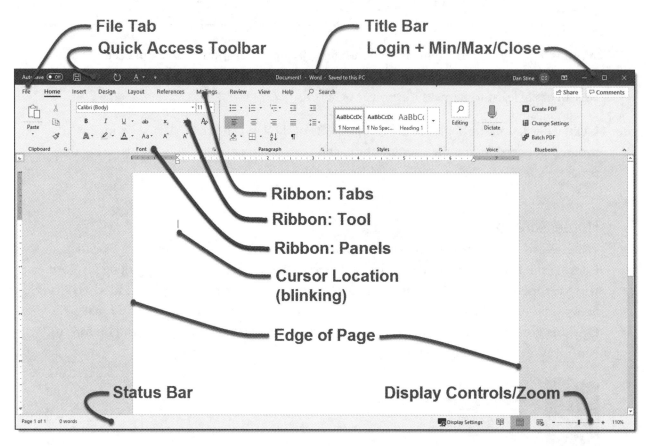

Word User Interface

Now, let's take a closer look at some aspects of the User Interface.

Application Title Bar

In addition to the *Quick Access Toolbar* and application controls, which are covered in the next few sections, you are also presented with the product name (Word) and the current file **name** in the center on the Application Title bar.

File Tab

Access to *File* tools such as *New, Open, Save, Save As, Share, Export* and *Print* and more. You also have access to tools which control the Word application as a whole, not just the current document, such as *Options* (see the end of this section for more on *Options*).

Quick Access Toolbar

Referred to as *QAT* in this book, this single toolbar provides access to often used tools: *AutoSave*, *Save*,
Undo, *Redo*. These tools are always quickly accessible, regardless of what part of the *Ribbon* is active.

The *QAT* can be positioned above or below the *Ribbon* and any command from the *Ribbon* can be placed on it; simply right-click on any tool on the *Ribbon* and select *Add to Quick Access Toolbar*. Moving the *QAT* below the *Ribbon* gives you a lot more room for your favorite commands to be added from the *Ribbon*. Clicking the larger down-arrow to the far right reveals a list of common tools which can be toggled on and off (see image to right).

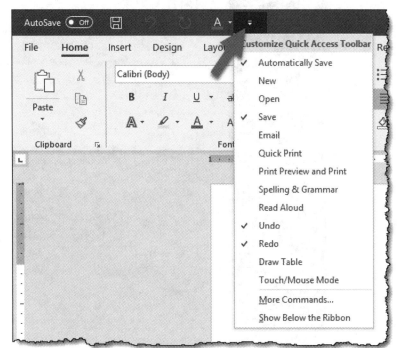

Ribbon – Home Tab

The *Home* tab, on the *Ribbon*, contains most of the word formatting & basic manipulation tools.

The *Ribbon* has three types of buttons: *button*, *drop-down button* and *split button*.

In the two following images, you can see the *Find* tool is a **split button**. Most of the time you would simply click the main part of the button to search for text in the current document. Clicking the down-arrow part of the button, for the *Find* tool example, gives you additional options: Advanced Find and Go To….

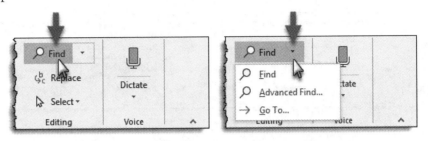

The next image is an example of a **drop-down button**. For this example, there is no dominant Select option provided. Rather, we are required to select from a list.

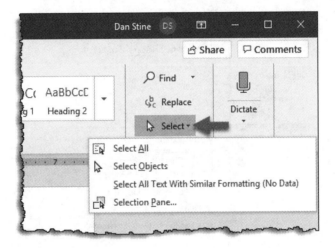

Ribbon – Insert Tab

To view this tab, simply click the label "Insert" near the top of the *Ribbon*. Notice that the current tab is underlined. This tab presents a series of tools which allow you to insert objects, images and more.

Ribbon – Layout Tab

The Layout tab controls the way document contents are displayed and printed.

Notice that some panels have a small icon in the lower right corner; for example, the Page Setup panel as shown in the image below. Clicking this icon opens a dialog with additional related options. This small icon is officially called a Dialog Box Launcher.

Ribbon – View Tab

The tools on the *View* tab allow you to toggle the Ruler and Gridlines on and off. Here you can also change the view type (e.g. Read Mode, Print Layout, etc.) and zoom the current document.

Ribbon – Add-in Tabs

If you install an **add-in** for Word on your computer, you will likely see a new tab appear on the Ribbon. Some add-ins are free while others require a fee. The image below shows two popular PDF writer/editor tools installed: Bluebeam and Adobe Acrobat.

Ribbon Visibility

The *Ribbon* can be displayed in one of two states:

- Full Ribbon (default)
- Minimize to Tabs

The intent of this feature is to increase the size of the available work area, which is helpful when using a tablet or laptop with a smaller display. It is recommended, however, that you leave the *Ribbon* fully expanded while learning to use the program. The images in this book show the fully expanded state. When using the minimized option, simply click on a Tab to temporarily reveal the tools. Click the Pin icon in the lower right to lock it open.

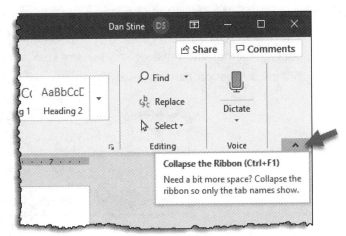

FYI: Double-clicking on a Ribbon tab will also toggle the Ribbon visibility.

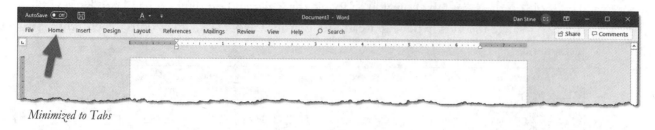

Minimized to Tabs

Temporarily Expanded

When using a tablet or touch screen, a Draw tab will also appear on the Ribbon. This is not required in the Word Associate exam, so just ignore it if you see it.

Status Bar

This area will display the current page number, total number of pages and words in the current document.

The right-hand side of the *Status Bar* shows the current zoom level and three display toggles: **Read Mode**, **Print Layout** (default) and **Web Layout**. The **Display Settings** button allows users with high resolution monitors (e.g. 4k) to toggle into compatibility mode if some Word add-ins do not support these displays. If an add-in does not support 4k screens (or Windows Text Scaling), their dialogs will be very small or parts will be jumbled and overlap, making the information hard to read.

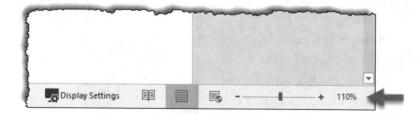

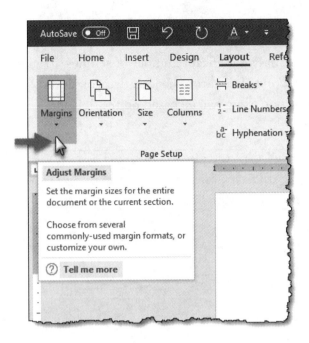

Hover your cursor over an icon for the tool name and a brief description of what it does as shown in the image to the right. Notice, there is also a link to the Help documentation via the **Tell me more** option.

Context Menu

The *context menu* appears near the cursor whenever you right-click on the mouse. The options on that menu will vary depending on what is selected, as shown in the two examples below (text selected on the left, an image on the right). Notice, the formatting toolbar also appears to facilitate quick adjustments, such as making text bold or a different color.

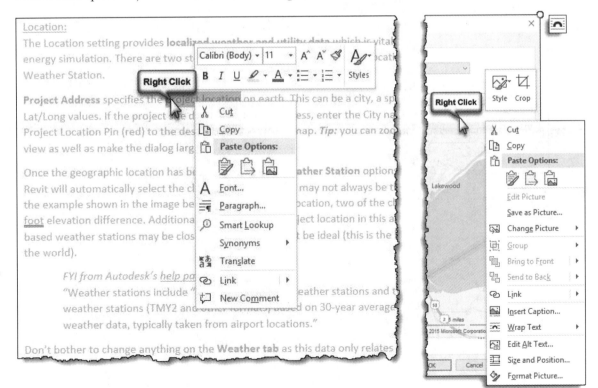

Word Options

The Options dialog, accessed from the File tab, has a significant number of settings, toggles and options used to modify how the program works. It is recommended that you don't make any changes here right now. The certification exam will be based on the default settings.

Efficient Practices

The *Ribbon* and menus are helpful when learning a program like Word; however, many experienced users rarely use them! The process of moving the mouse to the edge of the screen to select a command and then back to where you were is very inefficient, especially for those who do this all day long, five days a week. Here are a few ways experienced Word operators work:

- Use the **Wheel** on the mouse to scroll vertically and press and hold the wheel button while moving the mouse to scroll horizontally and/or vertically.

- Word conforms to many of the Microsoft Windows operating system standards. Most programs, including Word, have several standard commands that can be accessed via keyboard shortcuts. Here are a few examples (press both keys at the same time):

  - Ctrl + S   Save   *Saves the current file*
  - Ctrl + A   Select All   *Selects everything*
  - Ctrl + Z   Undo   *Undoes the previous action*
  - Ctrl + X   Cut   *Cut to Windows clipboard*
  - Ctrl + C   Copy   *Copy to selected content to the clipboard*
  - Ctrl + V   Paste   *Paste clipboard contents at cursor location*
  - Ctrl + P   Print   *Opens print dialog*
  - Ctrl + N   New   *Create new file*
  - F7   Spelling   *Launch spell check feature*

- Many Word commands also have keyboard shortcuts. Hover your cursor over a button to see its tooltip and shortcut (if it has one). In the example shown below, press **Ctrl + Return** to insert a page break at the cursor location.

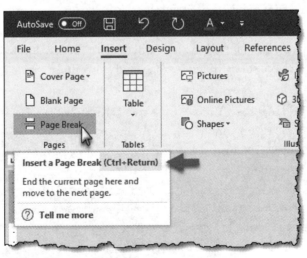

Keyboard shortcuts dialog

This concludes your brief overview of the Word user interface.

0.2 Certification Introduction

In the competitive world in which we live it is important to stand out to potential employers and prove your capabilities. One way to do this is by passing one of the Microsoft Certification Exams. A candidate who passes an exam has credentials from the makers of the software that you know how to use their software. This can help employers narrow down the list of potential interviewees when searching for candidates and reviewing resumes.

When the exam is successfully passed a certificate may be printed and displayed at your desk or included with your resume. You also have access to a Microsoft badge for use on business cards or on flyers promoting your work.

The exams <u>are</u> based on a specific release of Word. It is important that you ensure your version of Word matches the version covered in this book, and the version of the exam you wish to take. Ideally, you will want to take the exam for the newest version to prove you have the current skills needed in today's competitive workforce.

Important Things to Know

Here are a few big picture things you should keep in mind:

- **Practice Exam**
  - The practice exam, that comes with this book, is taken on **your own computer**
  - You need to have **Word installed** and ready to use during the practice exam
  - You must download the practice exam software from SDC Publications
    - See inside-front cover of this book for access instructions
  - **Required files** for the practice test
    - Files are downloaded with practice exam software
    - You do not need to know where these files are located
  - Note which questions you got wrong, and study those topics

- **Microsoft Word (Microsoft 365 Apps and Office 2019) - Exam**
  - Purchase the **exam voucher** ahead of time
    - If you buy it the day of the test, or at the test center, there may be an issue with the voucher showing up in your account
    - Note: some testing locations charge an extra proctoring fee.
  - Make a **reservation** at a test center; walk-ins are not allowed
  - A computer is provided at the test center
  - Have your Certiport **username** and **password** memorized (or written down)
  - If you fail, note which sections you had trouble with and study those topics
  - You must wait 24 hours before retaking the exam

Benefits

There are a variety of reasons and benefits to getting certified. They range from a school/employer requirement to professional development and resume building. Whatever the reason, there is really no downside to this effort.

Here are some of the benefits:

- Earn an industry-recognized credential that helps prove your skill level and can get you hired.
- Develop your skills with sample projects and exercises that emphasize real-world applications.
- Accelerate your professional development and help enhance your credibility and career success.
- Boost academic performance, prepare for the demands of a job, and open doors to career opportunities.
- Display your Microsoft certificate, use the Microsoft Certified badge, highlight your achievement and get noticed.

Certificate

When the exam is successfully passed, a certificate signed by Microsoft's CEO is issued with your name on it. This can be framed and displayed at your desk, copied and included with a resume (if appropriate) or brought to an interview (not the framed version, just a copy!).

Badging
In addition to a certificate, a badge is issued. Badging is a digital web-enabled version of your credential by **Acclaim**, which can be helpful to potential employers. This is a quick proof that you know how to use the Word features covered by the 365/2019 Associate exam.

Certified Specialist, Expert *and* Master

While this study guide focuses solely on the **Word Associate** exam, it is helpful to know about the other options for future consideration. There are seven different exam options. These are all paid options, not free, but when considering the value outlined previously, it is worth it. See the links at the end of this section to learn more about costs.

Associate	Expert	Master
Excel	Excel Expert ---------->	Excel Expert
Word*	Word Expert ---------->	Word Expert
PowerPoint ------------------------------->		PowerPoint
Access		Access *or* Outlook
Outlook		

* = Covered in this book

Microsoft Word (Microsoft 365 Apps and Office 2019) certification
Microsoft Word (Microsoft 365 Apps and Office 2019) certification is an excellent way for students and professionals to validate their software skills.

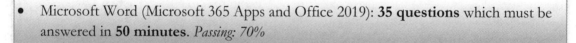

- Microsoft Word (Microsoft 365 Apps and Office 2019): **35 questions** which must be answered in **50 minutes**. *Passing: 70%*

Additional Microsoft Office certifications

In addition to the Microsoft Word (Microsoft 365 Apps and Office 2019) certification, which this study guide is based on, these are the other options and their format.

- PowerPoint: There are 35 questions which must be answered in 50 minutes.
- Excel Expert: There are 26 questions which must be answered in 50 minutes.
- Word Expert: There are 26 questions which must be answered in 50 minutes.
- Access: There are 31 questions which must be answered in 50 minutes.
- Outlook: There are 35 questions which must be answered in 50 minutes.

A special "Master" designation is earned if **both Expert** (Word & Excel) are passed along with the **Outlook** and **PowerPoint** _or_ **Access** exams.

All exams are live in-the-application style questions.

Exam Topics and Objectives

The Microsoft Word (Microsoft 365 Apps and Office 2019) exam covers six main topics. The outline below lists the specific topics one needs to be familiar with to pass the test. The remainder of this book expounds upon each of these items. In fact, this is the outline for each of the remaining chapters.

1. **Manage Documents**
   - Navigate within documents
   - Format documents
   - Save and share documents
   - Inspect documents for issues

2. **Insert and Format Text, Paragraphs, and Sections**
   - Insert text and paragraphs
   - Format text and paragraphs
   - Create and configure document sections

3. **Manage Tables and Lists**
   - Create tables
   - Modify tables
   - Create and modify lists

4. **Create and Manage References**
   - Create and manage reference elements
   - Create and Manage reference tables

5. **Insert and Format Graphic Elements**
   - Insert illustrations and text boxes
   - Format illustrations and text boxes
   - Add text to graphic elements
   - Modify graphic elements

6. **Manage Document Collaboration**
   - Add and manage comments
   - Manage change tracking

Exam Releases (including languages)

The **Certiport** website lists which languages and units of measure the exam & practice tests are available in as partially shown in the image below. For the full list, follow this link: https://certiport.pearsonvue.com/Educator-resources/Exam-details/Exam-releases

Microsoft Office Specialist (MOS)

✓+ = Recently Released   ✓ = Released

"Date" = Planned Release Date

"Blank" = Unavailable/Undetermined

"GMetrix" or "MeasureUp" = Practice test

Note: You may need to scroll right to see all of the languages.

MOS (Microsoft 365 Apps and Office 2019) Exams   MOS 2016 Exams   MOS 2013 Exams

MOS 2010 Exams

Microsoft Office Specialist (Microsoft 365 Apps and Office 2019) Exams

Product		ENU	ARA	CHS	CHT	DEU	ELL	ESM	FRA	IND	ITA	JPN	KOR	MAY	NLD	PLK	PJ
Word	Exam	✓+	✓+	✓+	✓+	✓+	✓+	✓+	✓+	✓+	✓+	✓+	✓+	✓+	✓+	✓+	✓
	GMetrix	✓+	✓+		✓+	✓+	Jan	✓+	✓+	✓+	✓+	Jan	✓+		✓+		Ja
Excel	Exam	✓+	✓+	✓+	✓+	✓+	✓+	✓+	✓+	✓+	✓+	✓+	✓+	✓+	✓+	✓+	✓
	GMetrix	✓+	✓+		✓+	✓+	Jan	✓+	✓+	✓+		Jan	Jan		✓+		Fe
PowerPoint	Exam	✓+	✓+	✓+	✓+	✓+	✓+	✓+	✓+	✓+	✓+	✓+	✓+	✓+	✓+	✓+	✓
	GMetrix	✓+	✓+		✓+	✓+	Jan	✓+	✓+	✓+		Feb	Feb		✓+		Fe
Outlook	Exam	✓+	✓+	✓+	Apr	✓+		✓+	✓+			Apr	✓+		✓+		
	GMetrix	✓+		Mar	Feb			✓+									
Word Expert	Exam	✓+		Jan	Feb	✓+		✓+	✓+			✓+	✓+				

Exam releases

Certified Training Centers

There are several places to take the exam. Many academic institutions administer the exam directly to their students. Additionally, there are formal testing facilities which offer a full range of similar exams, from Yoga Instructor certification to Senior Pharmacy Technician certification.

To find the nearest testing center, start here: http://portal.certiport.com/Locator

Unfortunately, there may not be a test center in your city. For example, the closest non-academic testing facility for the author of this study guide is 150 miles away. In this case, you will have to plan a day to travel to the testing center to take the exam. In this case it is much more important to have made an appointment, purchased the voucher ahead of time and associated it with your Certiport account… and of course, studied the material well, so you do not have to retake it.

Locating a training center

From the **Certiport** frequently Asked Questions (FAQ) online page:

> "Educators and students can take the exams at a public Certiport Authorized Testing Center or become a center themselves.
>
> If schools or districts want to run exams onsite, they can easily become a testing center and run the exams seamlessly in class. Institutions can sign up to be centers on the Certiport site."

Practice Exam (included with this book)

Practice exam software is included with this book which can be downloaded from the publisher's website using the **access code** found on the inside-front cover. This is a good way to check your skills prior to taking the official exam, as the intent is to offer similar types of questions in roughly the same format as the official exam. This practice exam is taken at home, work or school, on your own computer. You must have Word installed and access to the provided sample files, to successfully answer the in-application questions.

This is a test drive for the exam process:

- Understanding the test software
- How to mark and return to questions

- Exam question format
- Live in-application steps
- How the results are presented at the exam conclusion

An example of the Word practice exam is shown in the image below. When the practice exam software is started, Word is also opened and positioned directly above. During the timed exam seven projects are presented, each consisting of a separate Word file in which five questions must be answered by modifying the current Word document. At the end, the practice exam software will grade and present the results for the exam.

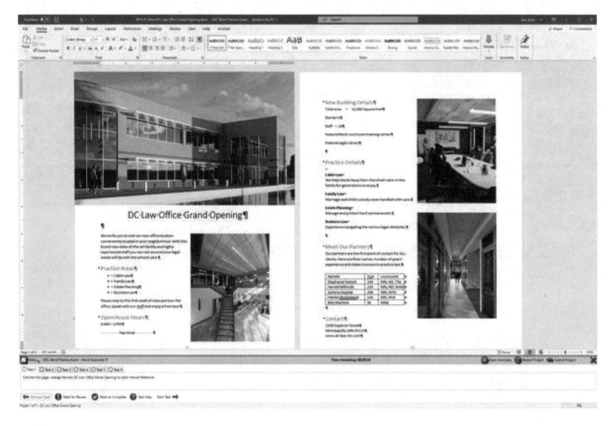

Included Practice Exam Software Example

Having taken the practice exam can remove some anxiety one may have going into an exam that may positively impact your career search.

See chapter 7 for more details on the Practice Exam software provided with this book.

Exam Preparation

Before taking the exam, you can prepare by working through **this study guide** and then the **practice exam**. You may also want to drive to the test location a day or so before the exam to make sure you know where it is and what the parking options are (if driving yourself) to ensure you are on time the day of the exam.

During the Exam

During the exam, be sure to manage your time. Quickly go through the test and answer the questions that are easy to you, skipping the ones you are not immediately sure of. The exam software allows you to view a list of questions you have not answered or have marked. Once you have answered all the easy questions you can then go back and think through those which remain. Do not exit the exam until you are completely finished, as you will not be able to re-enter the exam after that point.

> During the exam, some Word functionality is disabled, such as Help.

Exam Results

Once the exam is finished you will receive notification of your score immediately. You must earn 700 points (out of 1000) to pass, but this is a scaled score based on weighted questions. Thus, 70% does not exactly equal a passing score. If you failed, you should note the objective areas you were not as strong in and study those areas more before taking the test again – see image below. Be sure to print your score report and take it with you to study – it is also possible to log into your Certiport account later and print it from home.

SECTION ANALYSIS	
Manage Documents	100%
Insert and Format Text, Paragraphs, and Sections	75%
Manage Tables and Lists	100%
Create and Manage References	100%
Insert and Format Graphic Elements	100%
Manage Document Collaboration	100%

FINAL SCORE	
Required Score	700
Your Score	945

OUTCOME	
Pass	✓

Retaking the Exam

If the exam is failed, don't worry as you can take it again – as soon as 24 hours later. If you have any doubt about your ability to easily pass the exam, consider purchasing a voucher that includes a reduced cost "retake" option.

In the event that you do not pass the exam, and you have purchased the retake option, a retake code will be emailed to you. You may re-take the exam after waiting 24 hours from the time your initial exam was first started. Retake vouchers must be used within 60 days of the failed exam.

Here is the currently posted retake policy for the certification exam:

- If a candidate does not achieve a passing score on an exam the first time, the candidate must wait 24 hours before retaking the exam.
- If a candidate does not achieve a passing score the second time, the candidate must wait 2 days (48 hours) before retaking the exam a third time.
- A two-day waiting period will be imposed for each subsequent exam retake.
- There is no annual limit on the number of attempts on the same exam.
- If a candidate achieves a passing score on an MOS exam, the candidate may take it again.
- Test results found to be in violation of this retake policy will result in the candidate not being awarded the attempted credential, regardless of score.

Resources

For more information visit these sites:

- Certiport:
  https://certiport.pearsonvue.com/Certifications/Microsoft/MOS/Overview
- Acclaim (Credly):
  https://www.youracclaim.com/
- Microsoft:
  https://www.microsoft.com/en-us/learning/certification-exam-policies.aspx

Certiport User Registration

Here are the steps to create a Certiport account, which is required to take the exam.

Start here: https://www.certiport.com/Portal/Pages/Registration.aspx

Follow the steps outline on the site. Once complete, you will be prompted to register your account with a certification program. **Important:** be sure to select the Microsoft option in this step, and not Autodesk, Adobe, etc. This is done on the **Program tab** per the image below, just click the **Register** button (to the right of Microsoft) to get started.

Register your account with a certification program

Once you click Register, you will be prompted to verify your personal information on a new page. Once you complete this information and click Finish you will receive a confirmation email stating you are enrolled in the Microsoft certification program like the one shown below.

Registration confirmation email from Certiport

1 Manage Documents

Introduction

Review essential aspects of Word: navigation, formatting, saving and inspecting documents.

1.0 Create documents

The process of learning how to use Microsoft Word starts with opening the application, which was covered in the previous chapter, and then creating a new document. This section covers the steps required to create a new document.

1.0.0 From templates

The most common way to start a new document is from a template. A template is a special version of a Word document with specific settings, such as margins, spacing, etc. It can also have text and graphics. For example, it might have a company name and logo for a letter template. The main thing to know about a template is that when opened, via the New command, a copy of the document is what is opened. This prevents the template from getting altered unintentionally.

Create a new document from a template:

1. Open Word (covered in the previous chapter)
2. Select a template by:
    a. Click a template shown across the top, Blank document is most common
    b. Or, Click More Templates to see more purpose-specific options
3. Save the new document
    a. Provide a file location and name

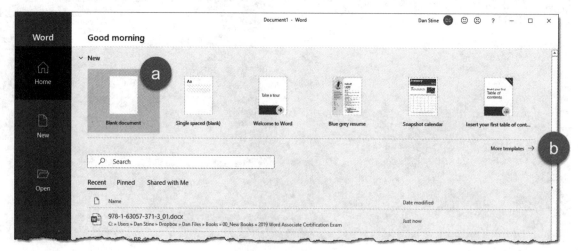

Create new document from template

1.0.1 From right-click in File Explorer

It is possible to create a new document outside of Word, within File Explorer. This method uses the Blank document template.

> **Tip:** An easy way to open Microsoft Windows **File Explorer** is by the following keystrokes on the keyboard: **Windows key + E** (just press the two keys at the same time).

Create a new document from right-clicking within File Explorer:

1. Within File Explorer, **right-click** in a blank area within a folder.
2. Click **New** in the menu.
3. Select **Microsoft Word Document**
   a. Provide a file name

Create new document from right-click in File Explorer

File extensions:

When opening Word documents, looking at its files on your computer, or preparing to copy them, it is helpful to know what the two *main* file extensions are.

- Word document   filename.**docx**
- Word template   filename.**dotm**
- Legacy document   filename.doc ('97 – 2003)
- Legacy template   filename.dot ('97 – 2003)

Note: By default, file extensions may not be showing within **File Explorer**. If desired, they may be turned on within File Explorer via View (tab) → Options → Change folder and search options → View (tab in dialog) → (uncheck) Hide extensions for known file types.

1.1 Navigate within documents

Knowing how to navigate within a document is important for efficiency and accuracy.

1.1.0 Open existing documents

Here are the steps to return to a previously created document.

Open an existing document:

1. Start Word, and then click **Open** on the left panel
2. Click **Browse**
3. In the Open dialog, browse to your document location, and **select it**
4. Click **Open**

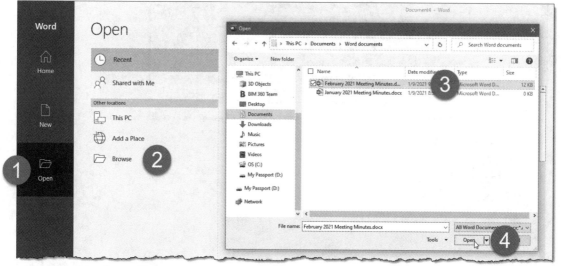

Open a previously created document

1.1.1 Search for text

Use the Find tool to search for text within the current document. The results, if any, are highlighted within the document and appear in context within the Navigation pane as shown in the image below. Clicking on one of the results listed will jump to that location.

Search for text using Find:

5. **Home → Find** (*or* **Ctrl+F**)
6. Enter text to search for, e.g. "career," and press Enter
7. The results are highlighted in the document

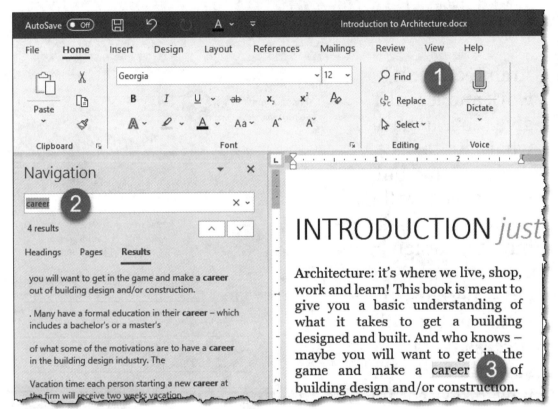

Search for text using Find

To search for text based on case, whole word and more, use Advanced Search.

Search for text using Advanced Find:

1. **Home → Find → Advanced Find…**
2. Enter text to search for, e.g. INTRODUCTION
3. Check desired options, e.g. Match case
4. Click the **Find Next** button: *each click advances to the next instance in the document*

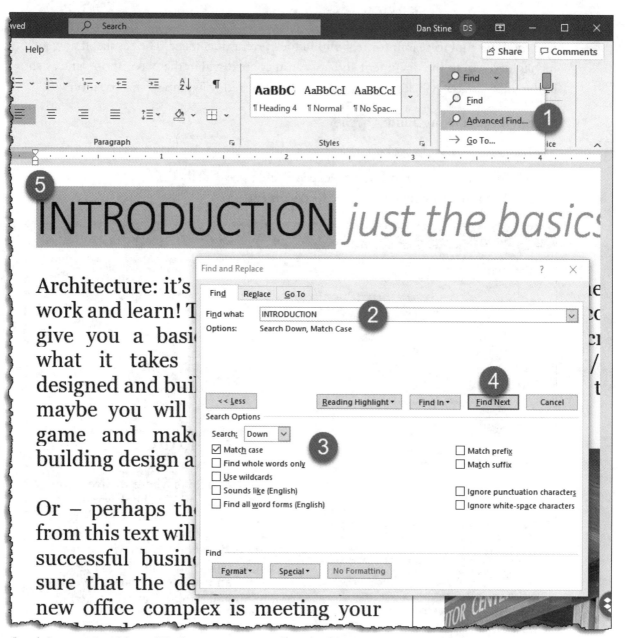

Search for text using Advanced Find

1.1.2 Link to locations within documents

Use the link tools to create a bookmark and cross-reference within documents.

Insert a bookmark:

1. Select text or click a location
2. **Insert → Bookmark**
3. Enter a name; *spaces are not allowed*
4. Click **Add**

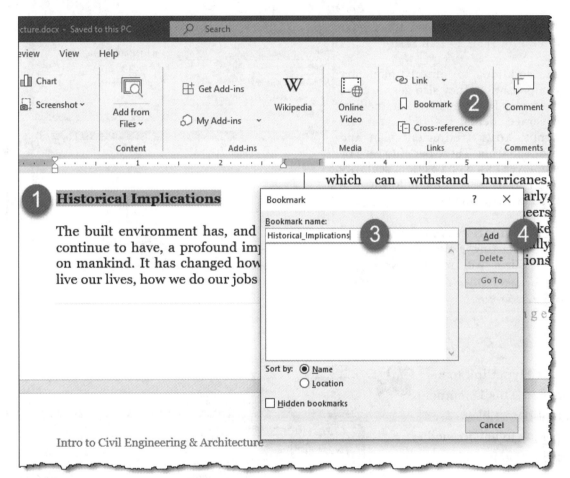

Add a bookmark

Insert a Cross-Reference:

1. Click a location
2. **Insert → Cross-Reference**
3. Select
    a. Reference type: *bookmark, table, etc.*
    b. Caption: *captions must already exist in document*
4. Click **Insert**

Use Ctrl+Click to jump to referenced data. Right-click link and Update Field if caption changes.

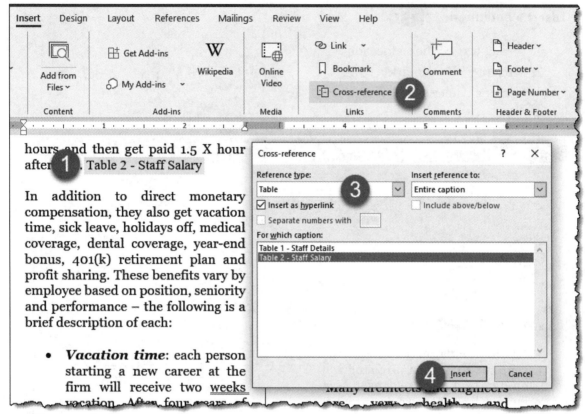

Add a cross-reference

Insert Hyperlink to a Place in This Document

It is also possible to use a hyperlink to link to another location within the same document.

1. Select text
2. Right-click
3. Select **Link…**
4. Click **Place in This Document**
5. Select an option: Headings or Bookmarks

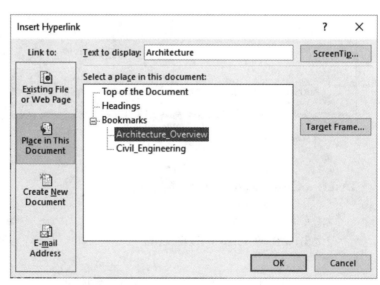

Link within document

1.1.3 Move to specific locations and objects in documents

Review the steps used to quickly jump to another location within the current document.

Use Go To: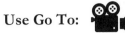

1. **Home → Find** (drop-down) **→ Go To…** (*or* **Ctrl+G**)
2. In the Find and Replace dialog:
    a. Reference type: *bookmark, table, etc.*
    b. Reference name: *reference must already exist in document*
3. Click **Go To**

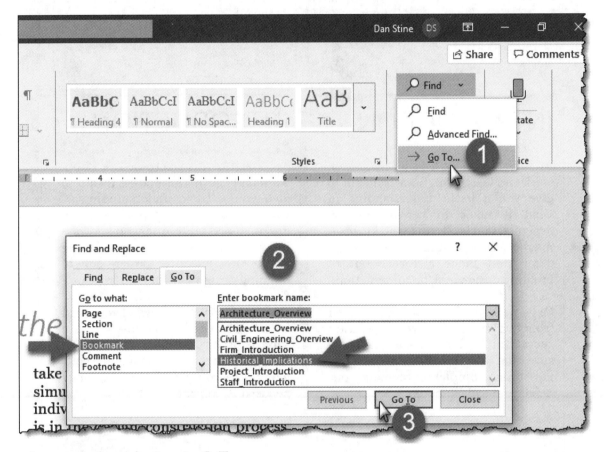

Jump to a bookmark location using Go To

1.1.4 Show and hide formatting symbols and hidden text

Show paragraph marks and other hidden formatting symbols, which help with page layout.

Use Show Hide ¶: 📹

1.   **Home →** ¶ (*or* **Ctrl+***) to toggle on
2.   Repeat step #1 to toggle off

▌ The keyboard shortcut is actually **Ctrl + Shift + ***

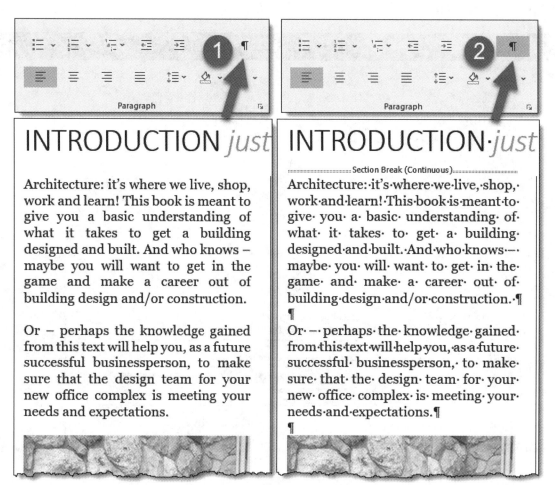

Toggle paragraph and hidden formatting symbols on and off

▌ In the context of Word, and the certification exam, each "paragraph symbol" defines a paragraph. For example, the exam may provide instruction on inserting something in the last paragraph. The last paragraph may not have any text associated with it, so be sure to toggle on the "paragraph symbol" visibility to make it easy to follow the instructions.

1.2 Format documents

Controlling formatting of a document is an important aspect of using Microsoft Word.

1.2.0 Moving the cursor around within document

In addition to moving to specific locations within a specific document, covered in the previous section, there are several efficient techniques to position the cursor within your immediate context. The current cursor location is where text is added then typing on the keyboard, as well as where symbols and graphics are inserted.

There are several ways to reposition the cursor from its current position:

Action	Cursor Result
Click mouse button	Moved to that location
Left Arrow	Move one-character left
Right Arrow	Move one-character right
Up Arrow	Move one line Up
Down Arrow	Move one row down
Ctrl + Left Arow	Move one word left
Ctrl + Right Arrow	Move one word right
Ctrl + Up Arrow	Move one paragraph up
Ctrl + Down Arrow	Move on paragraph down
Home	Move to beginning of line
End	Move to end of line
Ctrl + Home	Move to beginning of document
Ctrl + End	Move to end of document
Page up	Scroll up equal to height of visible page
Page Down	Scroll down equal to height of visible page
Ctrl + Page Down	Move to beginning of previous page
Ctrl + Page Down	Move to beginning of next page

1.2.1 Set up document pages

To define how a page looks, adjust the Margins, Orientation and Size. The Page Setup dialog has an array of options used to control how a page appears and prints to PDF or hardcopy.

Margins

Most printers cannot print to the edge of the page. Thus, margins are used to define the non-printable area at the perimeter of the page. <u>To set margins:</u> simply select from the predefined list on the **Layout** tab or click **Custom Margins...** to access the **Page Setup** dialog.

Setting margins for a page

Orientation

The orientation of a page can either be **Portrait** (vertical) or **Landscape** (horizontal) as shown below. Deciding which to use can be a personal preference, company standard or required based on the information (text and graphics) to be presented.

1. **Layout → Orientation → Portrait** *or* **Landscape**

Setting orientation for a page

Changing the orientation of a non-empty page may require some reformatting. In the example below, notice the image captions have moved and one page has more white space.

Comparing portrait (left) and landscape (right) page layouts

Size

The size of the page (aka paper) is set on the Layout tab.

1. **Layout → Size** (drop-down list)
2. Select an option:
    a. Pick from predefined list of page sizes, *or*
    b. Select **More Paper Sizes...** to open Page Setup dialog
3. Enter custom page size (optional)
    a. Allowable range is **0.1" – 22"**, thus, 22" x 22" is the largest page possible

Setting paper size

Columns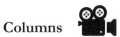

Define the number of columns from the Layout tab.

1. **Layout → Columns** (drop-down list)
2. Select an option:
    a. Pick from predefined list, *or*
    b. Select **More Columns…** to open Columns dialog
3. Specify Column options (optional)

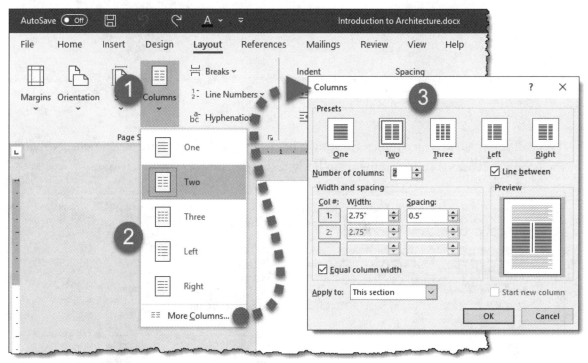

Setting number of columns

Comparing page layout for one, two and three columns

1.2.2 Apply style sets

Applying a style set can quickly change the look of the entire document.

A. **Design → Document Formatting gallery** (click down-arrow to see full list)

Apply a style set

Three different style set examples are shown below, applied to the same document. Notice the heading, captions and even the main body text style and formatting change.

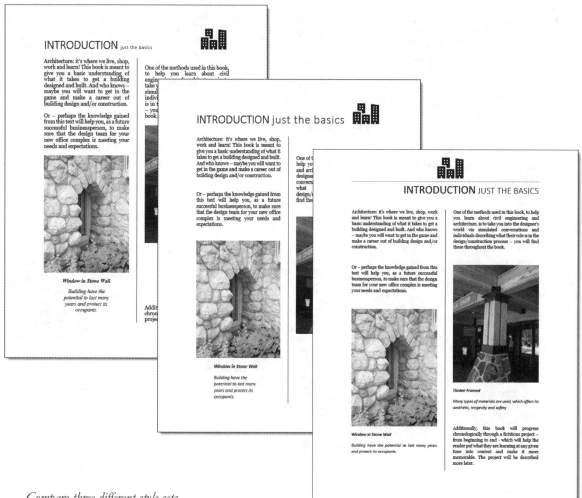

Compare three different style sets

1.2.3 Insert and modify headers and footers

Use headers and footers to display information to be repeated on each page, such as page number, chapter title and more. The related tools are found on the Insert tab.

Header and Footing tools on Insert tab

A) Insert Header

1. **Insert → Header** (list)
2. Select option:
   - **Built-in** option, *or*
   - Custom via **Edit Header**

B) Modify Header

1. **Insert → Header** (list)
2. Edit Header

C) Delete Header

1. **Insert → Header** (list)
2. Remove Header

The previews, for the built-in options shown to the right, are how they will appear when applied to your document. Often, it is more efficient to select a built-in option and then edit it, rather than starting a new one from scratch.

Built-in

Blank

[Type here]

Blank (Three Columns)

[Type here]   [Type here]   [Type here]

Austin

[Document title]

Banded

[DOCUMENT TITLE]

Facet (Even Page)

Facet (Odd Page)

🌐 More Headers from Office.com   >

📄 Edit Header

📄 Remove Header

📄 Save Selection to Header Gallery...

Header tools

A) Insert Footer

1. **Insert → Footer** (list)
2. Select option:
   - **Built-in** option, *or*
   - Custom via **Edit Footer**

B) Modify Footer

1. **Insert → Footer** (list)
2. Edit Footer

C) Delete Footer

1. **Insert → Footer** (list)
2. Remove Footer

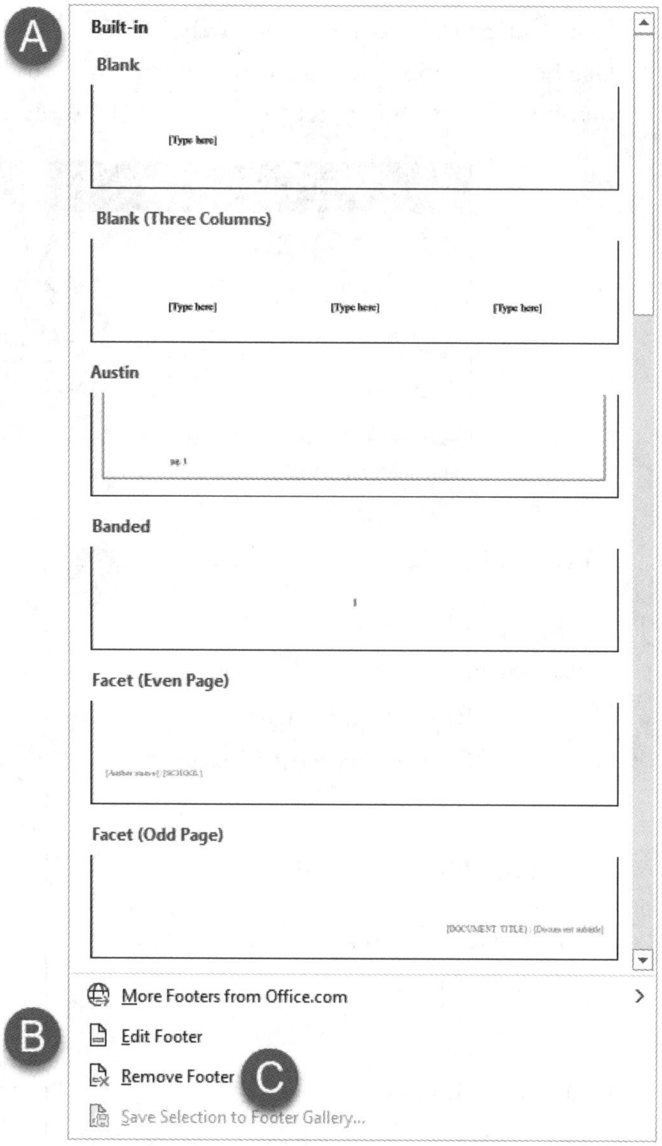

Ribbon Options

While in 'edit mode' for a header/footer, the Ribbon has some related options as shown below. These tools are also found in Page Setup.

- Different odd and even:
  For example, chapter title on one page and the book title on the next.

- Different first page:
  Unique first page, which could mean no header/footer at beginning of chapter.

- From Edge:
  Moves header/footer relative to edge of page but does not affect the margins.

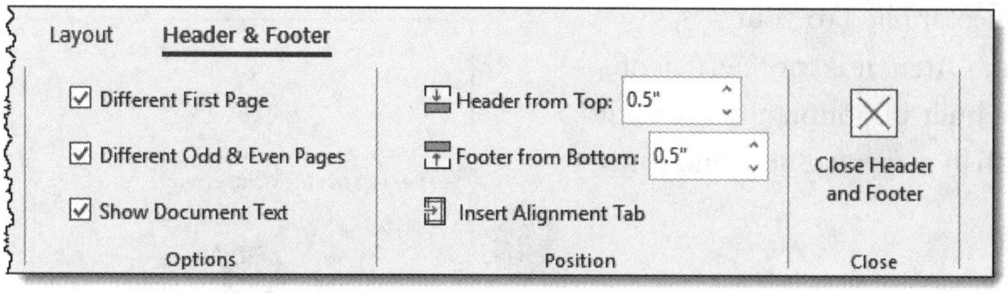

Footer tools

Ribbon tools while in header/footer edit mode

1.2.4 Configure page background elements

Review how to control the background color, text and page borders from the Design tab.

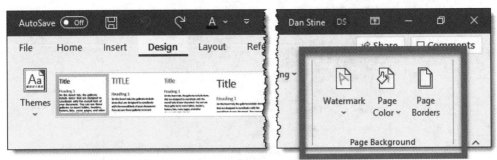

Page background tools on the design tab

Watermark

A watermark is text or an image that is transparent and is positioned behind the content in your document.

A) Insert Watermark

1. **Design → Watermark** (list)
2. Select option:
   - **Built-in** option, *or*
   - Custom via **Custom Watermark**

B) Custom Watermark

1. **Design → Watermark** (list)
2. Custom Watermark…
3. Printer watermark dialog (see next page)
   - Picture watermark: *browse for image*
   - Text watermark: *enter custom text*

C) Delete Watermark

1. **Design → Watermark** (list)
2. Remove Watermark

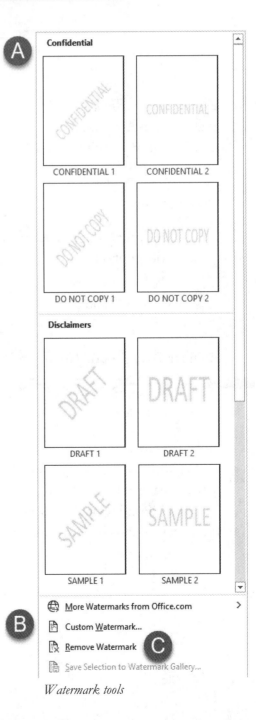

Watermark tools

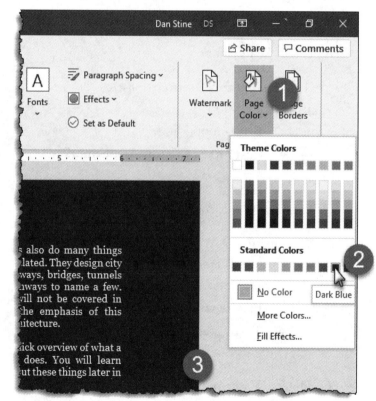

Custom watermark settings

Page Color

Selecting a page color fills the entire page background with that color.

Set Page Color

1. **Design → Page Color** (list)
2. Select option:
   - **Select a color**, *or*
   - More Colors

Remove Background Color

1. **Design → Page Color** (list)
2. No Color

Note: By default, background colors/images <u>do not print</u>. This may be changed here: Options → Display → Printing options: *Toggle*, Print background colors and images.

Set Page Color

Page Borders

Add a border to frame a page. The border is added within the margins, so they print.

Define a Page Border

1. **Design → Page Borders**
2. Select option:
   - Select a **Setting**, e.g. None, Box, Shadow, 3-D
   - Pick a line Style, Color, Width and/or Art option.
   - Preview area: pick one or more edges to toggle the border on/off

Remove Page Border

1. **Design → Page Border**
2. Click **None** (setting) and then **OK**

Define a page border

1.3 Save and share documents

Word documents may be shared directly, by saving to an alternative format and/or printing. This section will cover these options.

1.3.0 Save and close documents

It is important to save document edits before closing it, to ensure work is not lost. Word will prompt to save if a document with unsaved changes is being closed.

Documents may be saved manually or in real-time via AutoSave.

AutoSave document

1. On the application titlebar, toggle **AutoSace** on

   Tip: Use caution when opening a document with the intention of making a copy. Use Save-As right away to avoid editing the original document.

Save document

2. On the application titlebar, click the Save icon to commit changes to storage.

   Tip: Use Ctrl + S as another efficient way to save the current document.

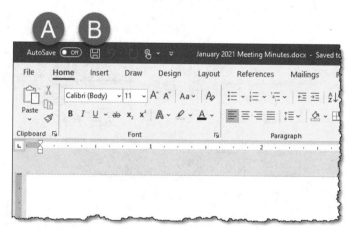

AutoSave and Save

Note: Documents opened from one of Microsoft's cloud-storage locations, such as OneDrive or SharePoint, will default to AutoSave mode.

Close document

Since each Word document is contained in a separate session of the application, simply click the **X** in the upper right to close the current document and the application.

Close the document and application

1.3.1 Save documents in alternative file formats

A Word document may be saved in several alternative formats, from legacy version of Word, for backwards compatibility, or a new Word template file for new documents (with or without macros enabled) to PDF and web page (html) formats to share with others who might not have word. Also, a PDF file preserves formatting and prevents editing.

Save document in alternate file format

1. Click the **File** tab on the Ribbon
2. Select **Save As**:
3. Select a file type from the drop-down list
4. Click the **Save** button

Save As options

The result of Save As is a new file, saved adjacent to the original file. To save to a different location, click the Browse button for step #3 and then specify a location, file type in the Save As dialog that opens.

1.3.2 Modify basic document properties

Each Word document has a place to enter unique properties used to track and identify it. These properties are also referred to as metadata and may be viewed without opening the file.

Modify document properties

1. Click the **File** tab on the Ribbon
2. Select **Info**
3. Select the **Properties** drop-down list and click **Advanced Properties**
4. Modify the document properties in the open dialog

When finished, to save the changes and return to the document, click the OK button and then the left-pointing arrow (in a circle) in the upper left

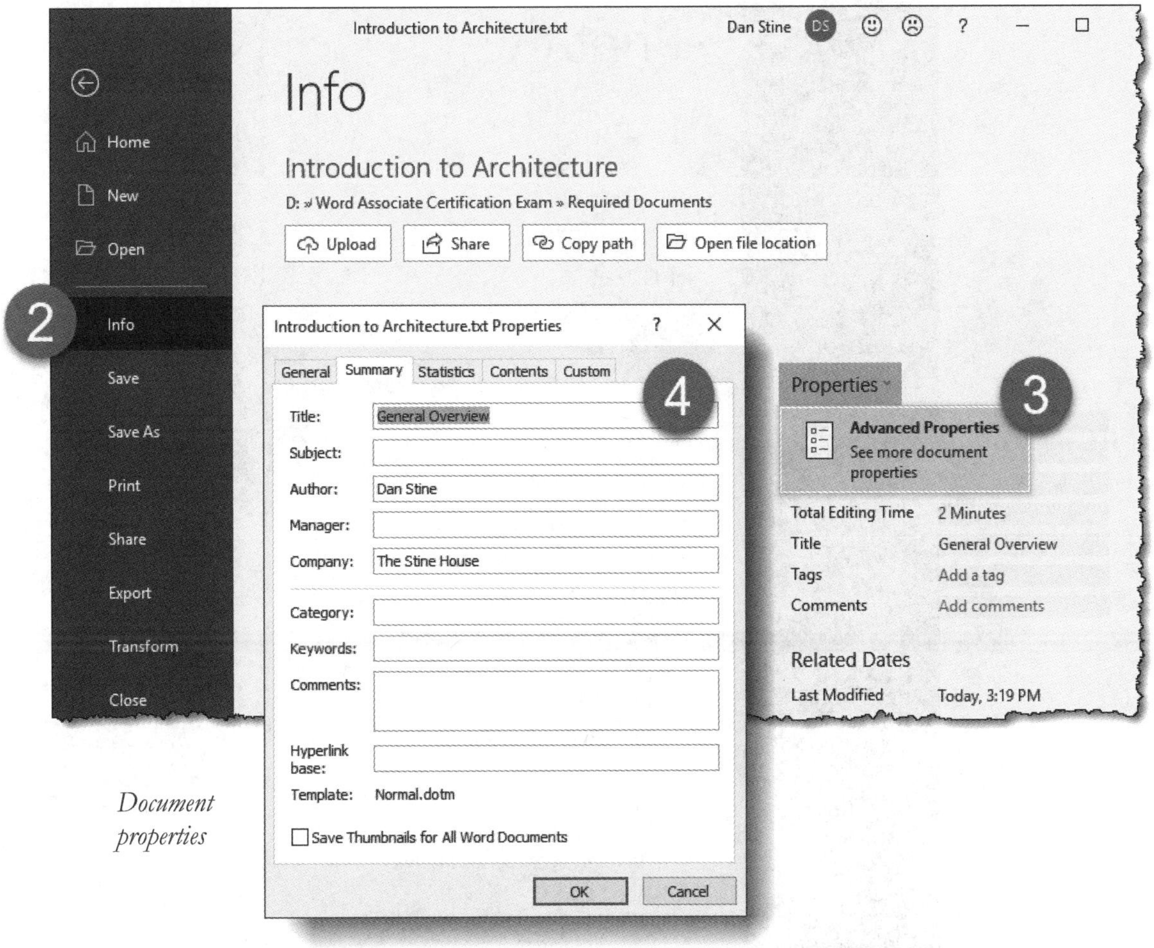

Document properties

This information can be made visible via Window's **file explorer** as shown here for "Authors".

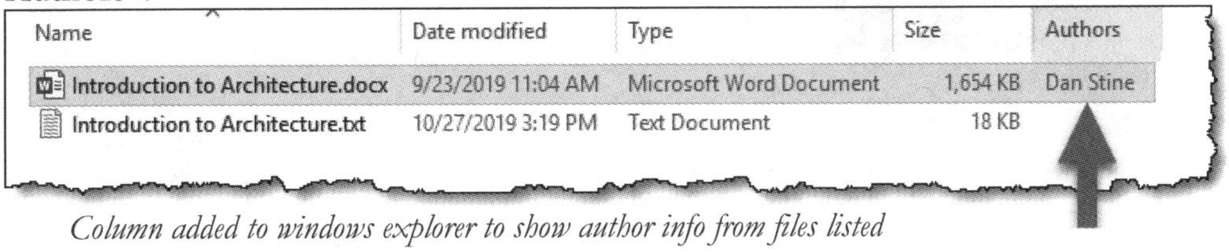

Column added to windows explorer to show author info from files listed

1.3.3 Modify print settings

Before sending a document to the printer, there are several settings which can be modified to change the layout and look of the printed page or PDF file.

Modify print settings

1. Click the **File** tab on the Ribbon
2. Select **Print**
3. Modify the print settings as desired

When finished, either click Print to send the document to the selected printer or click the left-pointing arrow, in the upper left, to return to the document.

Modify print settings for current document

1.3.4 Share documents electronically

Files can be shared electronically via OneDrive (cloud storage) or as an email attachment.

Share document electronically

1. Click the **File** tab on the Ribbon
2. Select **Share**
3. Select an option:
   a. OneDrive (cloud storage)
   b. Email: Word Document
   c. Email: PDF

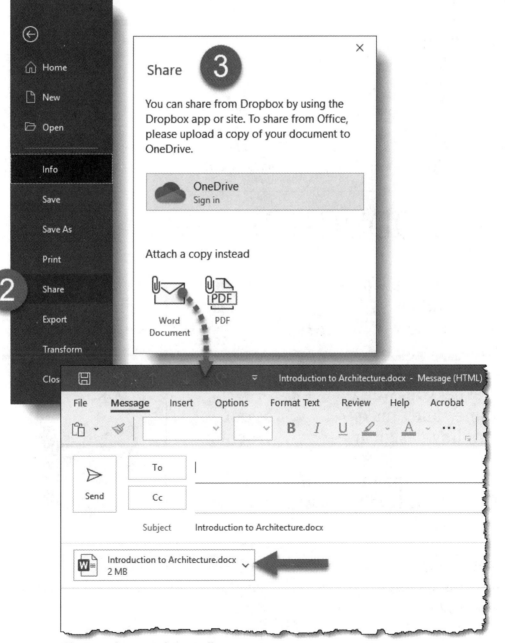

Sharing a document electronically

1.4 Inspect documents for issues

Before publishing a document, check to see what personal information it might contain, if it may be difficult for a person with a disability to read, or if it contains any features not supported by older versions of Word.

1.4.0 Spelling and grammar corrections

It is important that final documents are free of spelling and grammar errors to avoid confusing the reader. By default, these mistakes are highlighted automatically. They may be corrected as you go, or revisited all at once, later.

Correct spelling errors

Spelling errors are identified by a red wavy underline below the misspelt word.

1. **Right-click** on the misspelt word
2. Hover over **Spelling**, in the menu
3. **Select** the correct spelling for the word in question

   Tip: Synonyms are listed below each suggested word.

Correct spelling error

When technical, or industry specific, words (e.g. Autodesk, or DropBox) are used, they will be marked as misspelled. Use **Add to Dictionary**, shown above, to avoid this distraction while editing.

Correct grammar suggestions

Grammar issues are identified by a dashed purple line below the mispelt word. Keep in mind that all grammar suggestions are not necessarily errors, or wrong.

1. **Right-click** on the grammar suggestion
2. Hover over **Formality**, in the menu; *word changes depending on type of issue*
3. Select an option if desired; this will change the text under consideration

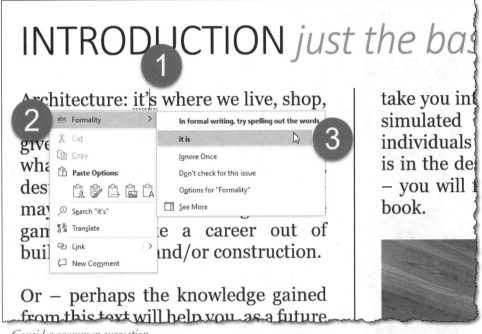

Consider grammar suggestion

Editor panel

The Editor panel is a way to look at all the spelling and grammar suggestions (see image to right). This panel is accessed from the **Editor** command on the **Review** tab.

Notice, the total number of suggestions listed at the top. In this example, there are no spelling errors: green checkmark. However, there are eight grammar issues to consider.

Clicking on the word Spelling or Grammar begins to step through the document to review each issue.

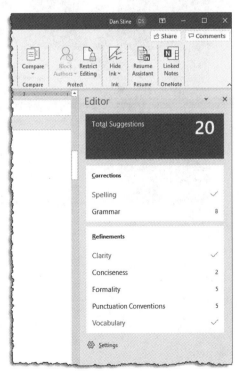

Editor panel – spelling and grammar

1.4.1 Locate and remove hidden properties and personal information

Check the document for hidden properties or personal information, with an option to 'Remove' for each section reported.

Check for hidden or personal information

1. Select the **File** tab on the Ribbon
2. Click **Info** on the left
3. Expand the **Check for Issues** list
4. Select **Inspect Document**

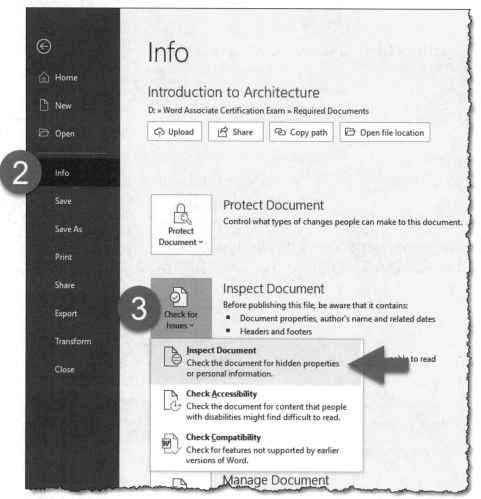

Check for hidden properties or personal information

After clicking Inspect Document, the following dialog is presented. Check the categories to inspect and then click the **Inspect** button.

Document categories to be inspected

A Remove All button appears in each category in which information exists. Click the Remove All button to delete the unwanted data from the document.

Results of inspecting a document's properties

1.4.2 Locate and correct accessibility issues

Check the document for content that people with disabilities might find difficult to read.

Check for accessibility issues

1. Select the **File** tab on the Ribbon
2. Click **Info** on the left
3. Expand the **Check for Issues** list
4. Select **Check Accessibility**
5. Review issues listed in the **Accessibility Checker** panel

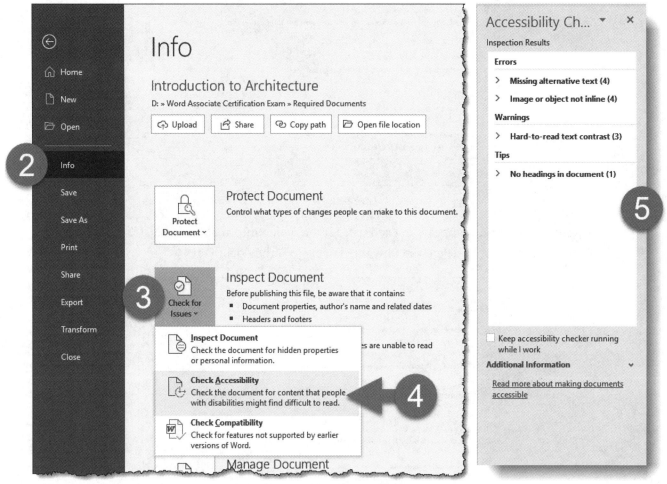

Check for accessibility issues

1.4.3 Locate and correct compatibility issues

Check for features not supported by earlier versions of Word.

Check for compatibility issues

1. Select the **File** tab on the Ribbon
2. Click **Info** on the left
3. Expand the **Check for Issues** list
4. Select **Check Compatibility**
5. Review results

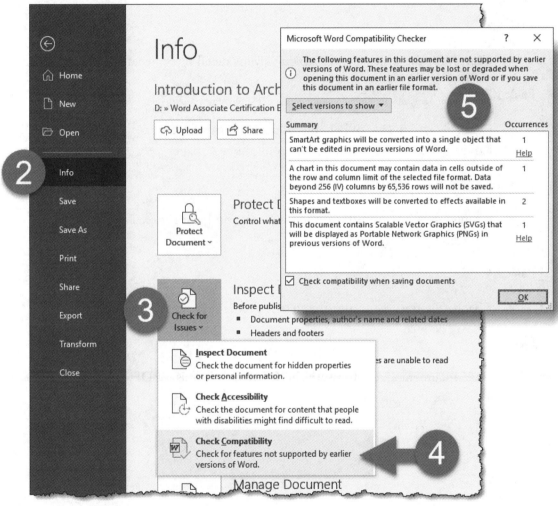

Check for compatibility issues

1.5 Practice tasks

Try the topics covered in this chapter to make sure you understand the concepts. These tasks are sequential and should be completed in the same Word document unless noted otherwise. Saving the results is optional, unless assigned by an instructor.

First Step:

✓ Open provided document **Introduction to Architecture.docx**

Task 1.1:

✓ **Search** for the word "dental" to quickly locate all three instances of the word.

Task 1.2

✓ On page 8, in the list of benefits, add an **internal reference** from the item "Dental Coverage" to the related description on the next page.

Task 1.3

✓ Change the **page orientation** to Landscape in Page Setup. The first page will not change.

Task 1.4:

✓ Change the document **margins** to the predefined Narrow option.

Task 1.5:

✓ Save document in an **alternate file format**; save it as a PDF.

1.6 Self-exam & review questions

Self-Exam:

The following questions can be used to check your knowledge of this chapter. The answers can be found at the bottom of the next page.

1. Word documents are commonly started from templates. (T/F)
2. The file extension for a Word document is .docx. (T/F)
3. The keyboard shortcut to search is Ctrl + S. (T/F)
4. Where is the Go To command found? _____.
5. Three columns are the maximum allowed. (T/F)

Review Questions:

The following questions may be assigned by your instructor to assess your knowledge of this chapter. Your instructor has the answers to the review questions.

1. The command to insert a Bookmark is on the ribbon's View tab. (T/F)
2. Margins can be customized. (T/F)
3. Changing the orientation of a page may require some reformatting of content. (T/F)
4. The largest page possible is 36" x 36". (T/F)
5. The Remove Footer command can be accessed from the Insert tab. (T/F)
6. Word can start a new email with the current document attached. (T/F)
7. Where are the document properties found? _____ .
8. Inspect Document helps make the document easier to read for people with disabilities. (T/F)
9. Background colors will always print by default. (T/F)
10. Page Border lines are positioned outside of the margins. (T/F)

Notes:

2 Insert and Format Text, Paragraphs, and Sections

Introduction

In this chapter you will review how to insert and format text, paragraphs and sections.

2.0 Manage text

Once text has been created, it then needs to be managed. This section will cover how to select, move, copy, and delete text.

2.0.0 Select text

Before text can be moved, copied, or deleted it must be selected. When text is selected, it is highlighted, as shown in the following example.

The people introduced might describe their role/position in the firm. Another method used to understand

Selected text

The most common way to select text and graphics is to position the cursor at the beginning, or left, and click and drag the mouse across the desired area to select—upwards or downwards. As shown in the table below, there are several other ways to quickly select text.

Ways to select text from the current cursor position:

Action	Selection Result
Click & drag mouse	Selects text and graphics
Shift + Left or Right Arrow	Selects one character at a time
Shift + Ctrl + Left or Right Arrow	Selects one word at a time
Double-click on word	Selects word, and any trailing spaces
Shift + Up or Down Arrow	Selects one line at a time, starting at cursor location
Single-click in left margin	Selects entire line
Ctrl + Click	Selects sentence
Triple-click	Selects entire paragraph
Ctrl + A	Selects entire document
Triple-click in left margin	Selects entire document

2.0.1 Move text

Selected text can easily be moved by dragging it. This is often preferred if the existing text, and its new location, are both visible on the screen/page.

Move text by dragging:

1. **Select** text
2. **Click** on selected text, **and drag** to desired location
3. Review results
   a. Use Undo (Ctrl + Z) if the results are not as expected

Move text

Move text by Cut and Paste:

This option is preferred/required as the existing text is on a different page/document than the desired new location. The previous image also applies to the following steps.

1. **Right-click** on the selected text, and select **Cut** from the pop-up menu (Ctrl + X)
   a. Note the text is now removed, and currently only exists in the clipboard
2. **Right-click**, at the desired location, and select one of the **paste options** (Ctrl + V)
   a. See table below for options
   b. The selected text is now moved
3. Review results

Paste Option	*Result*
Use Destination Theme (H)	Match document Theme set on Design tab
Keep Source Formatting (K)	Formatting applied to copied text is retained
Merge Formatting (M)	Only emphasis formatting retained, e.g. bold, italic
Picture (U)	Office 365 only; converts selected text to an image
Keep Text Only (t)	Source formatting, and non-text elements, discarded

2.0.2 Copy text

Selected text can be copied to another location in the same document, or to another Office document. As the name implies, the original text remains intact. When text is cut or copied, it is saved in the Office clipboard, which is lost when the computer is turned off.

Copy text using the clipboard:

1. **Select** the text to be copied
2. **Right-click** on the selected text, and select **Copy** from the pop-up menu (Ctrl + C)
3. **Right-click**, at the desired location, and select one of the **paste options** (Ctrl + V)
4. **Review** the results; the temporary menu allows the paste option to be changed

Copy text

Review results of copied text

2.0.3 Delete text

Deleting text is simple, but there are a few tips that are helpful to know.

Delete text:

1. **Select** text, or graphic elements, to be deleted
2. Press the **Delete** key, on the keyboard

Note that Cut text, not pasted anywhere, becomes deleted text.

Use **Undo** (Ctrl + Z) to restore deleted text. This is only possible while the document is open. Once it is closed, it is not possible to restore deleted text within a document. Thus, a backup strategy is recommended. Most companies have a backup system, where files are saved to an alternate location. Based on available backup space and time, files can be restored from previous days, weeks, months, and even years.

Backups

Note that cloud-storage is not necessarily a backup system. For example, if you have a Word document in OneDrive or DropBox and you edit it in that location, there is likely no backup to restore from. This is because storage and backup storage are two different things, with the latter requiring special setup and, often, an additional financial investment.

Files can be backed up manually. With the files closed, copy the file(s) to another location. Ideally, the backed-up files are stored in two physically different locations; for example, on a local computer and in the cloud.

Windows Previous Versions

Microsoft Windows has a feature called Previous Versions for personal computers and servers. When this feature is pro-actively setup, a file or folder can be restored from within File Explorer. Simply right-click on the file/folder, select Properties, and then selected the Previous Versions tab.

2.1 Insert text and paragraphs

This section will cover using find and replace, as well as how to insert symbols and special characters.

2.1.0 Enter text

Click to position the cursor and type on the keyboard to enter text.

2.1.1 Find and replace text

Review how to find and replace text in the current document.

Find text:

1. **Home → Find**
2. Enter text, e.g. "client," to find in the **Navigation** panel and press **Enter** to find all text

The results are listed below and highlighted in the document. The results, in the Navigation panel, are shown in context. Clicking an item here will jump to that location within the document.

Find text via the Navigation panel

Replace text:

1. **Home → Replace**
2. Enter:
   a. **What to find**, e.g. Client
   b. **Replace with**, e.g. customer
3. Optional: click the **More >>** button

Find and replace dialog and extended options

There are two 'replace' options:

- **Replace:** Replaces one instance at a time, in the order found
- **Replace All:** Replaces all occurrences in the entire document.

Clicking the **More >>** button offers more refined search options, such as **Match case**, where client, Client and CLIENT are not the same. Or, **Find whole word only**, where client, clients and clientele are not the same.

2.1.2 Insert symbols and special characters

Know how to insert symbols and characters not found on your keyboard.

Insert symbols and special characters:

1. **Insert → Symbol**
2. Either:
   a. Select a Symbol to insert at the cursor location, or
   b. Click **More Symbols**, to open the Windows Symbol dialog
3. Optional: select from the Symbols or Special Characters tab and then click the Insert button.

Changing the *Font*, on the Symbols tab, offers many additional symbol options.

Inserting a symbol or special character

2.2 Format text and paragraphs

This section reviews steps required to format text and paragraphs.

2.2.0 Apply text formatting

The formatting of selected text can easily be adjusted in Word. This includes the font, height, and emphasis (bold, underline, italic). These commands are prominently displayed in the Font panel on the Home tab of the Ribbon.

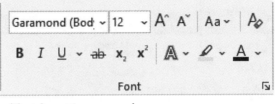

Text formatting commands

Ways to format selected text:

Command	Function
Font	Select font; see 'font variety', note below
Font Size	Adjust font size, whole/half numbers starting at 6
Increase Font Size	Makes text larger by one (Ctrl + Shift + >)
Decrease Font Size	Makes text smaller by one (Ctrl + Shift + <)
Bold	Toggles **bold** on or off (Ctrl + B)
Italic	Toggles *italic* on or off (Ctrl + I)
Underline	Toggles <u>underline</u> on or off
Strikethrough	Toggles ~~strikethrough~~ on or off
Font Options dialog	Additional options (Icon in lower right of Font panel)

Font variety

The available fonts can vary depending on installed applications and purchased font packs. For example, if Adobe Creative Cloud apps are installed, there will be additional fonts available for use on this computer, even in Office products. Keep in mind these fonts are copywritten and may not be available on other computers.

2.2.1 Apply text effects

In addition to traditional formatting, such as underline, italics and bold, there are several text effects which can be applied to text in Microsoft Word.

Apply Text Effects:

1. **Select** the text to be modified
2. Click **Home → Text Effects and Typography** drop-down list
3. Either:
   a. Pick a predefined effect style near the top of the menu, or
   b. Make a more specific change via the fly-out options below

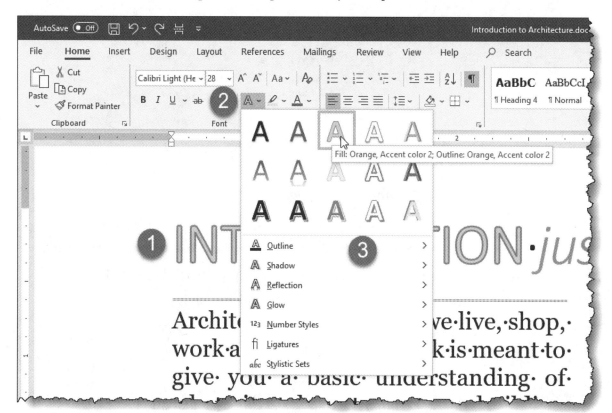

Apply text effect settings to selected text

An example of Reflection and Shadow are shown to the right, respectively.

Note: Text Effect is non-destructive, meaning the text is still text, not converted to an image, so spellcheck still works, for example.

Text effect: Reflection

Text effect: Shadow

2.2.2 Apply formatting by using Format Painter

Use the Format Painter to quickly apply the settings for the selected text to another part of the document—things like underline, bold, italic, font and color as applied.

Use Format Painter:

1. **Select** the text style to match; at least one character
2. Click **Home → Format Painter** (see tip below)
3. Select text to reformat
4. Review results

> Double-click the Format Painter button to apply the selected formatting to multiple locations; press the Esc key or another command when finished.

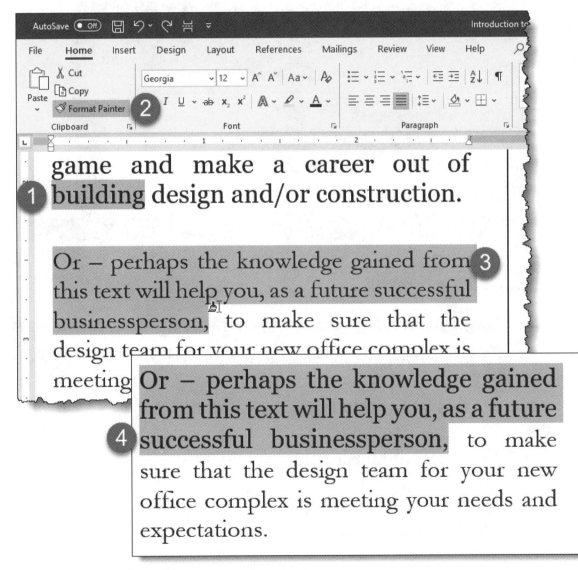

Using format painter to change text to match another

2.2.3 Set line and paragraph spacing and indentation

Review the steps required to set line and paragraph spacing as well as indentations.

Set Line and Paragraph Spacing:

1. **Select** the text to be modified, or Ctrl + A to select entire document
2. Click **Home → Line and Paragraph Spacing** drop-down list
3. Select a spacing option, e.g. 2.0
4. Review results

> The Column dialog has its own spacing controls; see section 2.3.1 below

In this example, the result is a double-spaced paragraph.

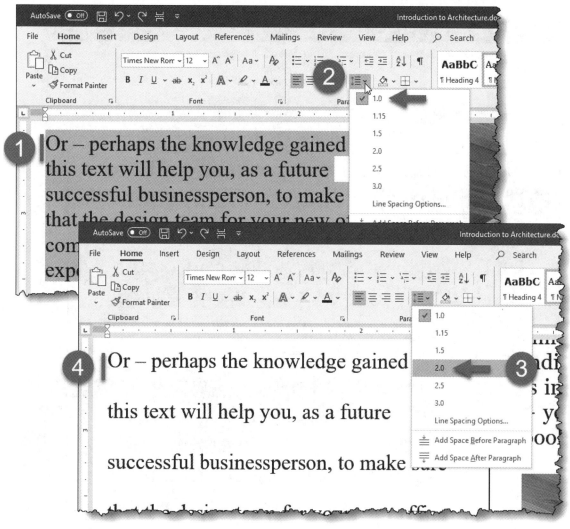

Modify the Line Spacing for Selected Text

In addition to the preset line spacing options, there are three additional options:

- **Line Spacing Options**: *see steps listed below*
- **Add Space Before Paragraph**: *adds a fixed amount of space before the selected paragraph*
- **Add Space After Paragraph**: *adds a fixed amount of space after the selected paragraph*

To specify a custom spacing value or to access additional options, such as indentation, use the **Line Spacing Options** to open the Paragraph dialog shown below. It is also possible to access this dialog via a right-click and selecting the Paragraph option in the pop-up menu.

Set Paragraph Indentation:

1. **Select** the text to be modified
2. Click **Home → Line and Paragraph Spacing → Line Spacing Options**
3. Modify the indentation settings, e.g. Left = 0.5"
4. Click **OK** and Review results

Notice, in this example, the paragraph is indented ½" from the left. This is in addition to the margins. Use the ruler, along the top of the page, as a quick accuracy doublecheck.

Modify the paragraph indentation for Selected Text

2.2.4 Apply built-in styles to text

Styles are used to create a consistent look by tying formatting to named styles. Changing a style definition changes all text referencing that style within the current document.

Applying a style to text:

1. **Select** the text to be modified
2. Click **Home → Styles, More** drop-down list
3. Select a built-in style option, e.g. *Intense Emphasis*

The selected text is now changed to match the settings for the selected style.

Applying built-in Styles to selected text

2.2.5 Clear formatting

Use Clear Formatting to reset the selected text to the default style; i.e. Normal.

Clear formatting:

1. **Select** the text to be modified
2. Click **Home → Clear All Formatting**

The Clear Formatting command is also located in the Styles list, as seen in the image on the previous page. This is the same command and produces the same result.

Clearing formatting for selected text

2.3 Create and configure document sections

The Word associate exam requires knowledge on creating and configuring document sections, which includes columns, page/section breaks and page setup option for a section.

2.3.0 Document section defined

A document section is defined by a Section Break and is used to segregate variations in formatting, headers/footers, etc. This reduces the need to maintain separate document files and facilitates automation, such as table of contents.

Some dialogs, like Custom Margins, allow changes to be applied to **current section** or **whole document**. *Tip:* Use the **Show/Hide Paragraph** toggle to see section breaks.

2.3.1 Format text in multiple columns

Learn to change the number of columns for a selection of text in the current document.

Section Breaks

Next Page
Insert a section break and start the new section on the next page.

Continuous
Insert a section break and start the new section on the same page.

Even Page
Insert a section break and start the new section on the next even-numbered page.

Odd Page
Insert a section break and start the new section on the next odd-numbered page.

Section break options

Apply column formatting:

1. **Select** the text to be modified; press Ctrl + A for entire document
2. Click **Layout → Columns** drop-down list
3. Select an option, e.g. *Two*

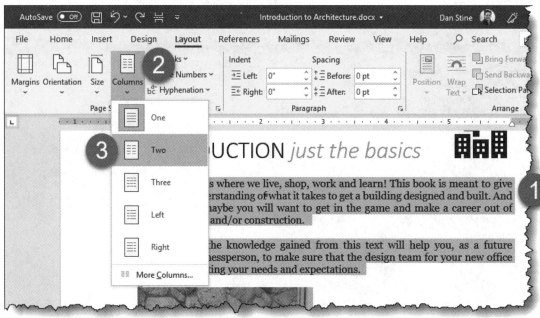

Applying column formatting

The selected text is now segregated into a new section and divided in the number of columns selected. In the following example, the Two column option was applied; with the default settings a vertical line is added between the columns.

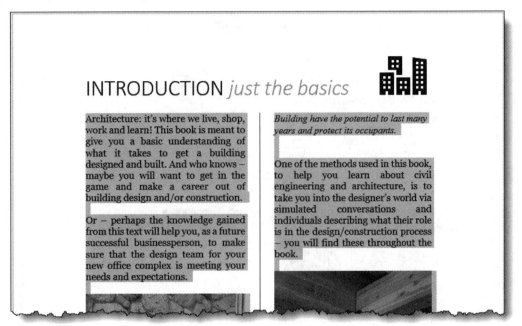

Two column formatting applied

For additional column formatting options, click the **More Columns…** option in the Columns drop-down list shown in the image on the previous page.

Note the following:

- **Number of columns**: enter a number greater than three
- **Line between**: check box
- **Width and spacing options** for each column; scroll bar appears for larger number of columns
- **Equal column width**: check box
- **Apply to**: Section text, Selected Sections, Whole Document

Columns options dialog

2.3.2 Insert page, section, and column breaks

Review the definition and steps to insert page, section and column breaks.

Insert page break: 🎥

In this example, a page break will be added so the heading text (and everything after it) will be forced to the next page.

1. **Click** to place cursor where page break is desired
2. Click **Layout → Breaks** drop-down list
3. Select **Page**
4. Review results

> Keyboard shortcut for page break is **Ctrl + Enter**

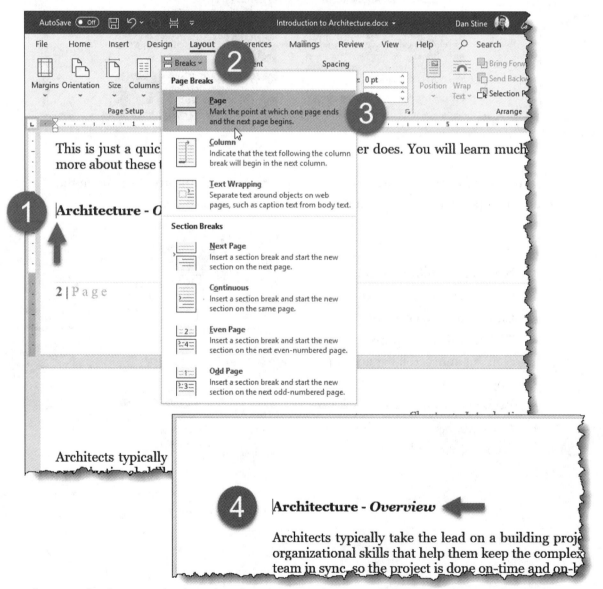

Insert page break at cursor location and result

Insert continuous section break:

A continuous section break allows the formatting to change on the same page. In this example, a continuous section break will be added to facilitate the transition to two columns on the same page.

1. **Click** to place cursor where continuous section break is desired
2. Click **Layout → Breaks** drop-down list
3. Select a **Section Breaks** option:
   a. Next Page: *starts a new section on the next page*
   b. **Continuous**: *starts a new section on the same page*
   c. Even Page: *starts a new section on the next even-numbered page*
   d. Odd Page: *starts a new section on the next odd-numbered page*
4. Review results

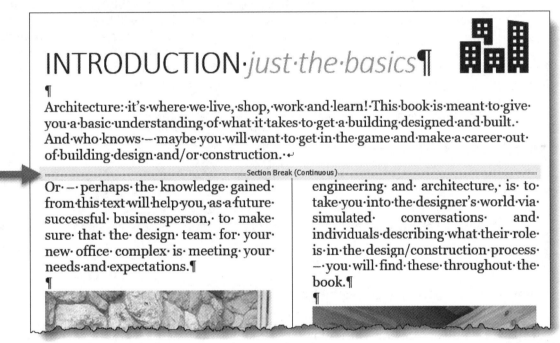

Insert continuous section break at cursor location and result

Section breaks facilitate formatting changes such as:
- Adding Columns
- Adding page numbering
- Adding a header or footer
- Changing page orientation
- Adding page borders

Insert column break:

Think of a column break as a section break within a section. This feature provides additional control over when a column ends and jumps to the next column.

1. **Click** to place cursor where column break is desired
2. Click **Layout → Breaks** drop-down list
3. Select **Column**
4. Review results

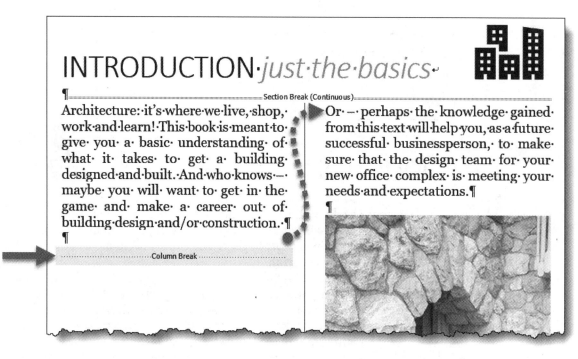

Viewing and Deleting page, section and column breaks:
Use the **Show/Hide paragraph marks** toggle (see image below) on the Home tab to make the page, section and column breaks **visible** within the document. An example of them being visible can be seen in the previous two images.

To **delete** a page, section or column break, first make them visible. Then, place your cursor just before a break and press the Delete key.

2.3.3 Change page setup options for a section

Page Setup options may be applied to the entire document or the current section. Know how to apply changes to a specific section.

Modify page setup options for a section:

1. **Click** to place cursor within a section to modify
2. Click the **Layout → Page Setup** dialog launcher icon
3. Verify 'Apply to' is set to **This Section**
   a. The 'This Section' option only appears when section breaks exist
4. Make desired changes on the Margins, Paper and/or Layout tabs
5. Click **OK** to apply the changes to the current section

Applying page setup changes to the current section

2.4 Practice tasks

Try the topics covered in this chapter to make sure you understand the concepts. These tasks are sequential and should be completed in the same Word document unless noted otherwise. Saving the results is optional, unless assigned by an instructor.

First Step:

- ✓ Open provided document **Introduction to Architecture.docx**

Task 1.1:

- ✓ **Find and Replace** all instances of the word "Typically" with "Usually".

Task 1.2

- ✓ Find the word "Specialized" and replace the "TM" **symbol** with the copyright symbol.

Task 1.3

- ✓ Apply text effect **Gradient Fill: Blue, Accent color 5; Reflection** to the word "Introduction" in the main title of the document.

Task 1.4:

- ✓ Set the **line spacing** of the first paragraph to 1.5.

Task 1.5:

- ✓ Apply the **built-in style** Quote to the second paragraph.

2.5 Self-exam & review questions

Self-Exam:

The following questions can be used to check your knowledge of this chapter. The answers can be found at the bottom of the next page.

1. Using Shift + Ctrl + Right/Left Arrow selects one word at a time. (T/F)
2. The Find command is located on the Review tab. (T/F)
3. The Font options are not the same on every computer. (T/F)
4. Keyboard shortcut for Undo? _____
5. The tool Text Effect results in the selected text being converted to an image. (T/F)

Review Questions:

The following questions may be assigned by your instructor to assess your knowledge of this chapter. Your instructor has the answers to the review questions.

1. Using Cut and Paste results in moving text. (T/F)
2. The Symbol command is located on the Design tab. (T/F)
3. The Format Painter cannot be used to modify multiple locations. (T/F)
4. The selected text's Line Spacing can be changed from the Home tab, without needing to open a dialog box. (T/F)
5. For consistency within a document, multiple text format adjustments can be grouped by using Text Styles. (T/F)
6. A paragraph indentation can be adjusted in the paragraph dialog box. (T/F)
7. Which key, on the keyboard, is used to remove the selected content? _____ .
8. The Page Setup dialog icon is found on the ribbon's Layout tab. (T/F)
9. The command to draw a line through the selected text? _____ .
10. Use the Ctrl + Enter to add a Page Break at the cursor location. (T/F)

Notes:

3 | Manage Tables and Lists

3.0 Introduction to tables and lists

Before learning how to create and manage tables and lists it is helpful to understand what they are, in the context of Word, and why they are needed.

3.0.0 Tables defined

Tables are mainly used to organize information, like how Microsoft Excel is used, but within a document that is primarily sentences. Notice the two examples below, where the text on the left is not aligned when using the same number of tabs on each line. It is possible to get the information to align but takes an ongoing effort. For example, everything could align until the last line, which requires going back and adjusting all previous lines by adding another tab.

Conversely, the table on example on the right will always align and can easily be adjusted by dragging the column spacing. Additionally, tables have formatting options to right align a column to, for example, align the decimal place in currency.

Monday	3:00 pm
Tuesday	9:00 am
Wednesday	10:00 am
Thursday	1:30 pm
Friday	12:00 pm
Saturday/Sunday	Closed

Monday → 3:00·pm¶

Tuesday → 9:00·am¶

Wednesday → 10:00·am¶

Thursday → 1:30·pm¶

Friday→12:00·pm¶

Saturday/Sunday → Closed¶

Data organized with tabs   *Data organized within a table*

3.0.1 Lists defined

Lists are used to organize a single column of information, such as steps, table of contents, ingredients, etc. The main options are Numbered or Bulleted. Numbered can be numbers, letters or a combination as shown in the two examples on the left, below. Bulleted lists use graphics, like the dot/circles shown below. A numbered list is preferred if the list represents a specific order. The **Decrease/Increase Indent** buttons are used to control line hierarchy.

A. Days of Operation
    a. Monday
    b. Wednesday
    c. Thursday
    d. Friday
    e. Saturday/Sunday

1. Days of Operation
    a. Monday
    b. Wednesday
    c. Thursday
    d. Friday
    e. Saturday/Sunday

• Days of Operation
    o Monday
    o Wednesday
    o Thursday
    o Friday
    o Saturday/Sunday

List examples

3.1 Create tables

Review the steps required to create tables in the current document.

3.1.0 Create tables from copy

One way to create a table is by copying an existing table from the current document or another open Word document. This might be done if using the same information in multiple documents, or if the formatting is the same. In the latter example, the text is modified, and the formatting is kept intact, which might save time for a heavily formatted table. Formatting might include shaded columns/rows, font variations, hidden/dashed lines, etc.

Copy a table:

1. Hover over a table
2. **Select the icon** that appears in the upper left (see arrow in image below)
3. Copy to clipboard using **Ctrl + C**
4. Position cursor at new location in current document or another open document
5. Paste from clipboard using **Ctrl + V**

Design team

Name	Role	Salary	Years of Experience
Rachel Johnson	Architect	$85k	8
Joe Billman	Structural Engineer	$80k	6
Martin Hepler	Civil Engineer	$110k	26
Sarah Burden	Mechanical Engineer	$94k	14
Ben Smith	Electrical Engineer	$90k	8

The copied table has no connection to the original table. Thus, changes to the new table will not affect the original table, and vice versa.

3.1.1 Convert text to tables

Previously typed text can be converted to a table, and even divided into separate columns.

Convert text to table:

1. Select the text to be converted
2. Click **Insert → Table** list
3. Click **Convert Text to Table…**
4. Select options in dialog, click **OK**
   a. Separate text at: **Comma**
5. Review results

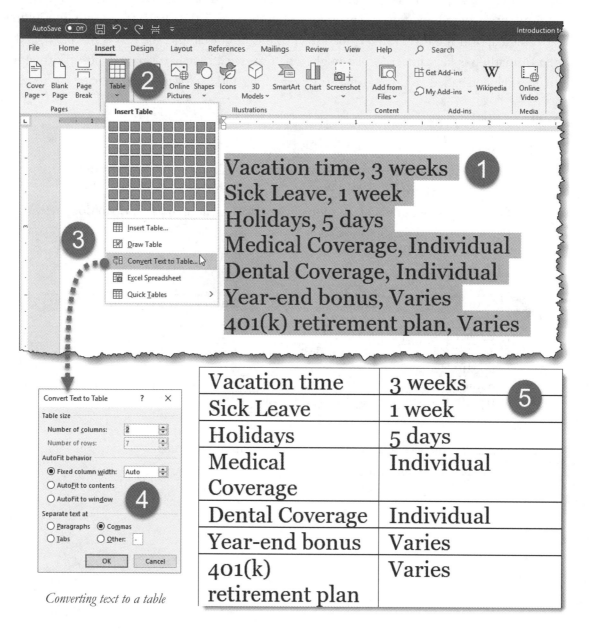

Converting text to a table

The **Convert Text to Table** dialog values are automatically set based on the selected text. In the previous example, Word noticed the **commas** and set that as the column separator, which then dictated the number of columns. It is possible to increase the **Number of columns** value, which results in additional blank columns.

▌ Additional rows and columns may be added later, after the table is created.

The example below has spaces separating the values to be divided into columns. In this case, the **Other** option was selected, and a **'space'** manually entered in the text box, within the Convert Text to Table dialog.

	Jones	21
	McGough	55
Abi	Johnson	45
Marty	Bennet	32
Rachel	Luck	43
Edward	Hanson	64

Bob Jones 21
Sarah McGough 55
Abi Johnson 45
Marty Bennet 32
Rachel Luck 43
Edward Hanson 64

Separate text at
○ Paragraphs   ○ Commas
○ Tabs   ◉ Other:

Converting text to a table

3.1.2 Convert tables to text

Tables can be converted to text, thus removing the table definition altogether.

Convert table to text:

1. Click anywhere within the table
2. Click **Layout → Convert to Text**
3. Specify how column data should be separated; e.g. **Comma**, click **OK**
4. Review the results

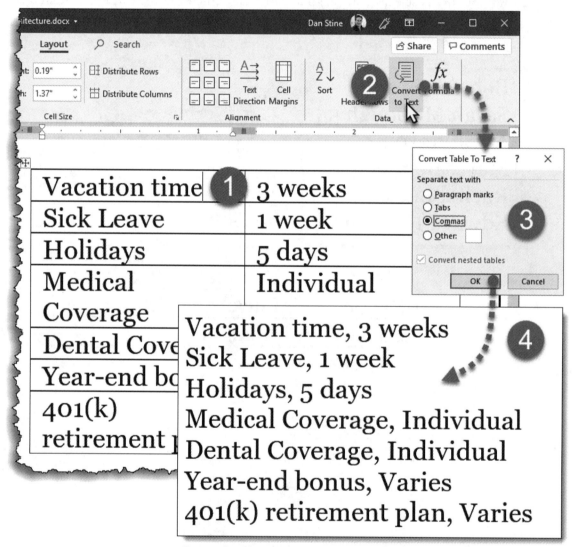

Converting table to a text

3.1.3 Create tables by specifying rows and columns

Review the steps required to create a new schedule with a specific number of rows and columns.

Create a new table:

1. Click to place the cursor where the table should be inserted
2. Click **Insert → Table** drop-down list
3. Do one of the following:
   a. Move the cursor across the cells to define the desired table size, or
   b. Click Insert Table and manually enter number of rows/columns

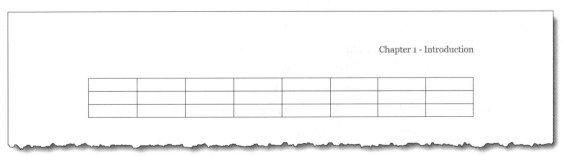

Creating a table – two options

The result is a blank table with the specified number of rows and columns, as shown below.

Empty new table created

3.2 Modify tables

Study this section to review steps required to modify tables.

3.2.0 Table design and layout tabs on the Ribbon

Once a table has been created there are many tools available to edit them. Before some of these workflows are covered, it is helpful to know how these tools are accessed.

Clicking within, or selecting, a table reveals two tabs on the Ribbon; they are:

- Table Design
- Layout

These tabs, and a portion of their contents, are shown in the following image.

Table Design and Layout tabs – shown when a table is selected

Some tools are applied to the entire table, like the table styles options. Others are applied to the selected portion of the table, such as a cell, row, or column.

Here is a little more detail about each tab:

Table Design
The tools on the Table Design tab are used to select a table style, table style options, and control how the lines making up the table look (i.e. borders).

Layout
The tools on the Layout tab facilitate inserting, splitting, and even deleting table cells, rows, and/or columns. Here, it is also possible to control the size of a cell, row, and/or column as well as the text justification. Finally, since information, or data, is nicely segregated within tables in Word, there are tools to work with this data, such as sorting, e.g. alphabetically, or adding formulas.

3.2.1 Sort table data

Sort data within a table, by column and in ascending or descending order. Using this method, the rows all move together to maintain data integrity; e.g. a person's first name will not separate from their last name when sorting by last name. The entire row is sorted, but just by last name.

Sort the contents of a table:

1. Click anywhere within a table
2. Click **Home → Sort**
3. Modify the Sort dialog:
   a. Select a column to sort by; e.g. **Column 2**
   b. Specify **Ascending** or Descending
   c. Select Header Row, if columns have a title that should not move
   d. Click **OK**; optionally, use the two **Then by** sections to sort by multiple columns
4. Review the results

Sorting the contents of a table

3.2.2 Configure cell margins and spacing

Review steps to modify a table's margins and spacing within each cell.

Modify cell margins and spacing:

1. Click anywhere within a table
2. Click **Layout → Cell Margins**
3. Modify the Table Options dialog (applies to each cell within the table):
    a. Adjust cell margins; e.g. **Left = 0.2"**
    b. Adjust spacing between cells; e.g. **0.01"**
    c. Click **OK**
4. Review results

Each cell now has a larger space on the left, and there is a gap between each cell, which introduced another set of lines within the table.

Modifying cell margins and spacing within a table

3.2.3 Merge and split cells

Cells within a table can be merged and split when needed.

Merge Cells:

1. **Click and drag** to select two or more continuous cells
2. Click **Layout → Merge Cells**
3. Review results

The selected cells, and their contents, are now combined into a single cell.

Merging two cells into one

The image to the right shows how merged cells might be used in a header. Notice two cells have been merged: name and age. In this example, text alignment has also been modified within each merged cell.

Name		
First	Last	Age
Marty	Bennet	32

Example of how merged cells might be used

Split Cells:

1. **Click** to select a cell
2. Click **Layout → Split Cells**
3. Modify the Split Cells dialog:
   a. Change Number of columns value; e.g. **2**
   b. Click **OK**
4. Review results

The selected cell is now split into two cells. The newly created cell can have unique data entered.

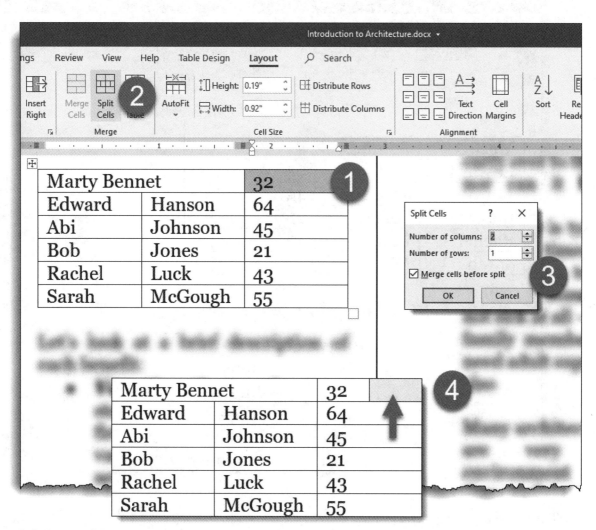

Splitting one cell into two

3.2.4 Resize tables, rows, and columns

Learn to resize tables, rows and columns in this section.

Resize table: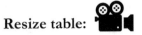

Follow these steps to resize the overall width of a table. Note that the overall height is defined by the cumulative height of the rows.

1. **Click** within a table to select it
2. Click **Layout → Properties**
3. In the Table Properties dialog, on the Table tab:
   a. **Check** preferred width
   b. Enter a width for the table; e.g. **2"**
   c. Click **OK**
4. Review the results

Modifying the overall width of a table

Resize rows: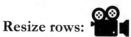

Follow these steps to resize the height of one or more rows.

1. **Click** to select one or more rows; e.g. row 1
   a. Click and drag to select multiple rows
2. Click in the **Layout → Height** textbox and enter a value; e.g. **0.4"**
3. Review the results

The second example below shows the result if all rows were selected.

Single row selected when editing row height value

Marty	Bennet	32
Edward	Hanson	64
Abi	Johnson	45
Bob	Jones	21
Rachel	Luck	43
Sarah	McGough	55

Multiple rows selected when editing row height value

Resize columns:

Follow these steps to resize the width of one or more columns.

1. **Click** to select one or more columns; e.g. column 3
   a. Click and drag to select multiple columns
2. Click in the **Layout → Width** textbox and enter a value; e.g. **0.5"**
3. Review the results

The second example below shows the result if all columns were selected at a width of 0.7".

Single column selected when editing column width

Marty	Bennet	32
Edward	Hanson	64
Abi	Johnson	45
Bob	Jones	21
Rachel	Luck	43
Sarah	McGough	55

Multiple columns selected when editing column width

3.2.5 Split tables

Word allows tables to be split, horizontally, into two tables.

Split table:

1. **Click** anywhere within a row
   a. The split will occur above this row
2. Select **Layout → Split Table**
3. Review the results

The table is now split into two tables. If the results are not as expected, click Undo (or Ctrl + Z) to revert to a single table and try again.

Splitting a table at the selected row

3.2.6 Configure a repeating row header

If the first row contains headers for each column, like the example below, then it may be desirable to toggle on Repeat Header Rows. When active, the header row will repeat at the top whenever the table extends onto another page or column.

Toggle repeating header rows on:

1. **Click** anywhere within a table to select it
2. Select **Layout → Repeat Header Rows** to toggle it on
   a. The button has a dark gray background when toggled on
3. Review the results

First	Last	Age
Bob	Jones	21
Marty	Bennet	32
Rachel	Luck	43
Abi	Johnson	45
Sarah	McGough	55
Edward	Hanson	64
Rachel	Johnson	25
Joe	Billman	34

First	Last	Age
Martin	Hepler	28
Sarah	Burden	51
Ben	Smith	18
Charlie	Bath	19
Kelly	Pollock	44
Barney	Trader	56
Manny	Gates	38

Header row automatically repeated for the given table

3.3 Create and modify lists

This section covers steps used to create and modify lists.

3.3.0 Starting a list using AutoCorrect

When starting a new list, before any text has been typed, an AutoFormat feature within Word can be used to streamline the process.

AutoCorrect options dialog

There are two options related to lists within the AutoCorrect options dialog. This is accessed from the **File** tab → **Options** → **Proofing** → **AutoCorrect Options…** button.

Automatic bulleted lists

- Creates a bulleted list when a line of text starts with *****, **-**, or **>** followed by a **space** or **tab**.
- To end a bulleted list, press **Enter** two times.

Automatic numbered lists

- Creates a numbered list when a line of text starts with the number **1** followed by a **period** or **tab**.
- To end a numbered list, press **Enter** two times.

Create a list using AutoFormat

3.3.1 Format paragraphs as numbered and bulleted lists

Creating numbered and bulleted lists is an important concept to know for the exam. Compare steps below with the image on the next page.

Format selection as numbered list:

Steps to create a numbered list, based on numbers and/or letters.

1. **Click and drag** to select multiple paragraphs
   a. In this case, a paragraph can consist of a single word
2. Select **Home → Numbering**
   a. See sub-topic B below for additional options
3. Review the results

Format selection as bulleted list:

Steps to create a bulleted list, based on symbols.

1. **Click and drag** to select multiple paragraphs
   a. In this case, a paragraph can consist of a single word
2. Select **Home → Bullets**
   a. See sub-topic A below for additional options
3. Review the results

Additional options:

The previous steps use the default bullet/number options. There are additional pre-defined bullets and numbering options as follows:

A. Click the down-arrow associated with the Bullets icon to see the built-in options shown on the next page. Select an option to apply to the current selection. This may be done while initially creating the list or to change an existing list.

B. Click the down-arrow associated with the Numbering icon to see the built-in options shown on the next page. Select an option to apply to the current selection. This may be done while initially creating the list or to change an existing list.

Applying bullets and numbering to selected paragraphs

If an extra Enter is pressed between each paragraph, then extra bullets would be added. It is best to use Word's paragraph spacing options to avoid this problem.

3.3.2 Change bullet characters and number formats

Learn to modify the symbol used for bullets and edit the formatting for numbered lists.

Change bullet characters:

Know how to change the symbol of a bulleted list.

1. **Click** anywhere within a bulleted list
2. Select **Home** → **Bullets** → **Bullet Library**; select an option
3. Review the results

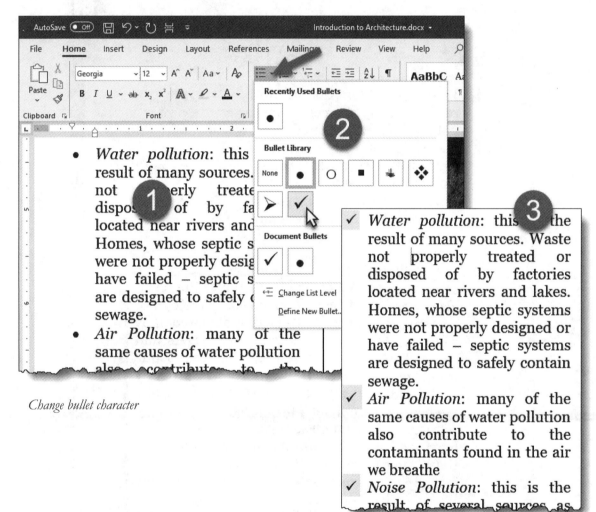

Change bullet character

Change number formats: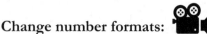

Review the steps required to modify the format of numbered lists.

1. **Click** anywhere within a numbered list
2. Select **Home → Numbering → List Library**; select an option
3. Review the results

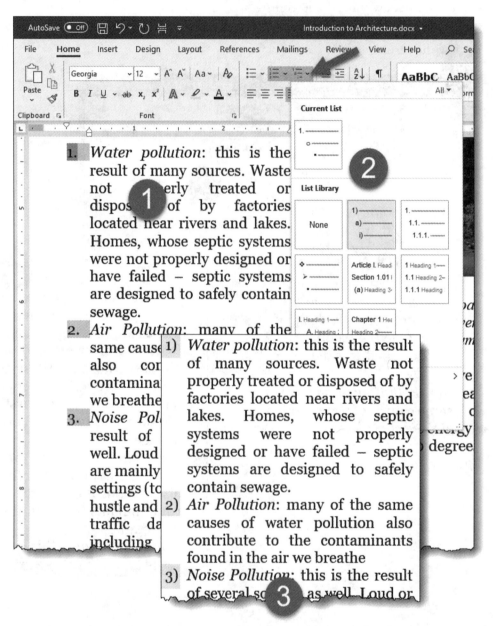

Notice the List Library also controls the symbol and format for indented items in the list.

3.3.3 Define custom bullet characters and number formats

Learn to modify the symbol used for bullets and edit the formatting for numbered lists.

Define custom bullet characters:

In addition to the built-in symbols covered in the previous step, custom options are available.

1. **Click** anywhere within a bulleted list
2. Select **Home → Bullets → Define New Bullet...**
3. Click the **Symbol...** button in the Define New Bullet dialog
4. Select a **Font** group and then a **symbol**, click **OK**
5. Review the results

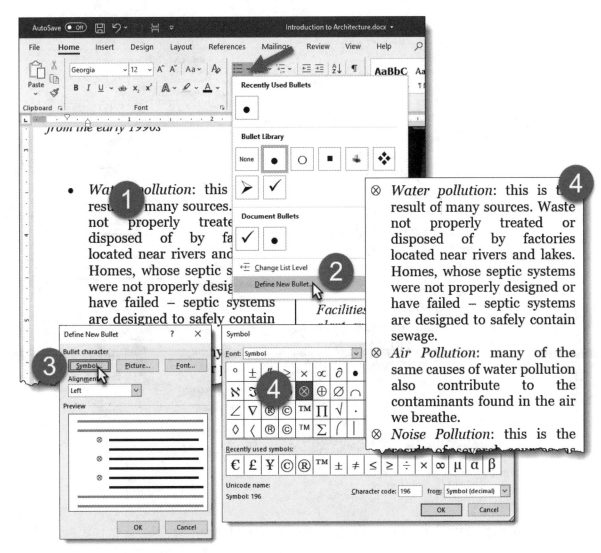

Defining a custom bullet symbol

Define custom number formats:

Review the steps required to define a custom format for numbered lists.

1. **Click** anywhere within a numbered list
2. Select **Home → Numbering → Define New Number Format…**
3. Modify style, format and/or alignment settings in the dialog box, click **OK**
4. Review the results

Defining a custom number format

> These custom definitions only apply to the current document.

3.3.4 Increase and decrease list levels

Know how to change the list level of a bulleted or numbered list.

Increase or Decrease the list level:

1. **Click** anywhere within a bulleted list
2. Do one of the following options:
    a. **Decrease indent**: Shift list item left and use next list level bullet/number
    b. **Increase indent**: Shift list item right and use next list level bullet/number
3. Review the results

The example below used **Increase indent** to shift the selected list item right, which changed the bullet symbol to the next level as defined in the current list format. For this same example, clicking **Decrease indent** would revert the list back to its original layout.

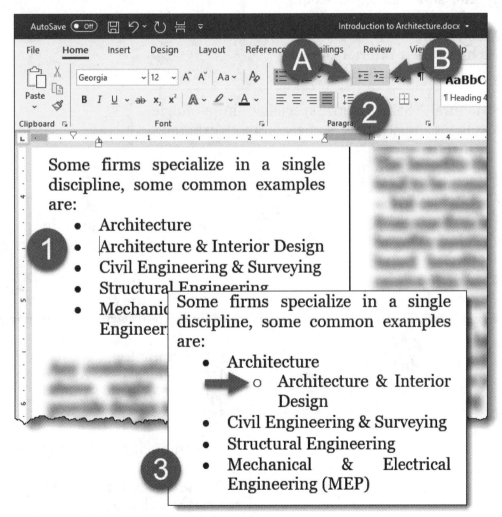

Changing the list level for a selected item in a list

3.3.5 Restart and continue list numbering

A portion of a list can be separated, or combined, from a previous segment.

Restart list numbering:

A list can be forced to restart at number 1 at any location. This is also helpful when starting/pasting a new list which automatically continues from a previous list.

1. **Right-Click** on the list item to restart at
2. In the pop-up menu, select **Restart at 1**
3. Review the results

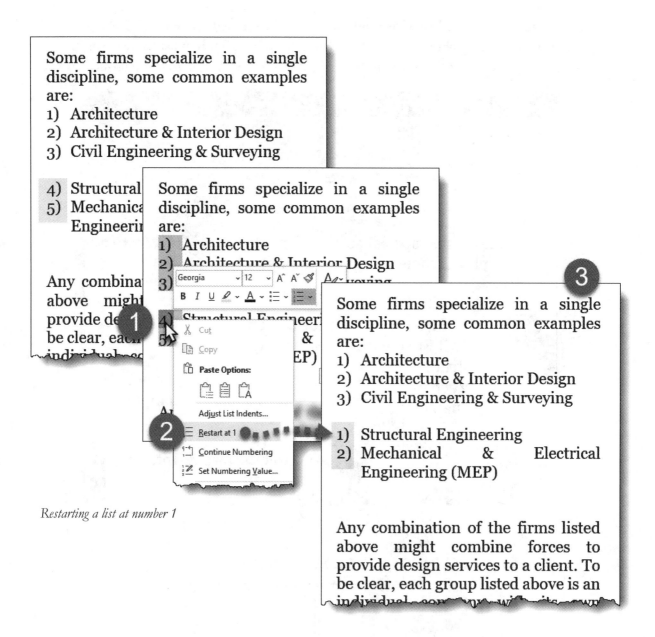

Restarting a list at number 1

Continue list numbering:

A list can be forced to continue numbering from a previous list, which may be on a previous page.

1. **Right-Click** on the list item to continue numbering at
2. In the pop-up menu, select **Continue Numbering**
3. Review the results

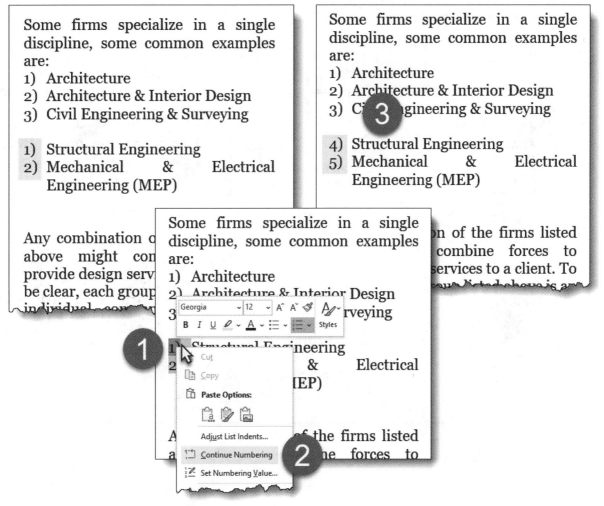

Continue list number from previous list

3.3.6 Set starting number values

The starting value of a numbered list can be changed to any number and does not need to be associated with a previous list.

Set numbering value:

1. **Right-Click** on the list item to change/set value
2. In the pop-up menu, select **Set Numbering Value…**
3. Enter a starting value; e.g. **22**
4. Review the results

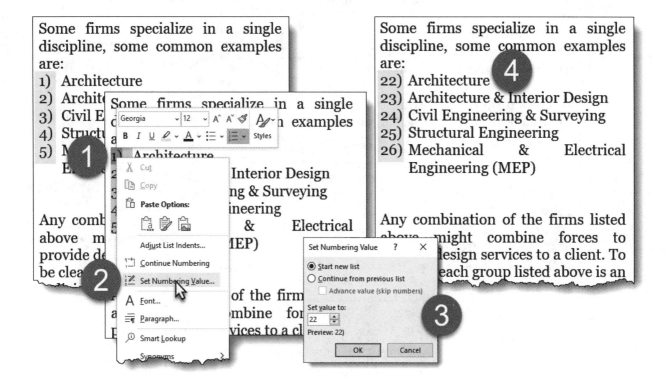

Setting the number value of a numbered list

3.4 Practice tasks

Try the topics covered in this chapter to make sure you understand the concepts. These tasks are sequential and should be completed in the same Word document unless noted otherwise. Saving the results is optional, unless assigned by an instructor.

First Step:

✓ Open provided document **Introduction to Architecture.docx**

Task 1.1:

✓ Convert the table at the end of the document to text, with tabs separating text.

Task 1.2

✓ Select the list of benefits on page 8, and format as bulleted list.

Task 1.3

✓ In the newly formatted bulleted list, increase the indent for Sick Leave and Dental Coverage.

Task 1.4:

✓ Change the bulleted list on page 7 to a numbered list starting at #3.

Task 1.5:

✓ At the end of the document, after the chart, create a 7 x 2 table: 7 columns, 2 rows.

3.5 Self-exam & review questions

Self-Exam:

The following questions can be used to check your knowledge of this chapter. The answers can be found at the bottom of the next page.

1. A 10 x 8 table is the largest you can make, by highlighting the squares in the Table drop-down, before needing to open the Insert Table dialog. (T/F)
2. The ribbon's Table Design tab appears whenever a table is in a document. (T/F)
3. Multiple columns, within a Table, cannot be sorted at once. (T/F)
4. The command to make a second list continue from the previous list? _____ _____.
5. A table's cell may not be split into two. (T/F)

Review Questions:

The following questions may be assigned by your instructor to assess your knowledge of this chapter. Your instructor has the answers to the review questions.

1. The Convert Text to Table commands is found on the ribbon's Insert tab. (T/F)
2. Table cells have their own margin settings. (T/F)
3. Height adjustments, on the Layout tab for a table, affect every row and cannot be applied to individual rows or just one. (T/F)
4. A table can be split into two separate tables. (T/F)
5. When a table spans multiple pages, the header row cannot repeat. (T/F)
6. It is possible to use a character from any font, as a custom bulleted list. (T/F)
7. The command, on the Layout tab, to combine two or more cells? _____ .
8. The first item in a numbered list cannot be made to start at a specified number, such as 22. (T/F)
9. Command to move a list item to the next level? _____ _____ .
10. Right-clicking on a numbered list and selecting Restart List will cause the list to begin from 1 at the selected location. (T/F)

4 Create and Manage References

4.0 Academic and formal reports

This section will introduce the tools and workflows Word offers to create formal reports.

4.0.0 Using Word to create compliant reports

When creating a formal report for school or within a professional environment it is well worth the time to learn the tools and workflows found on the References tab within Word.

One will find a lot of automation and tools to create and manage complex documents. From table of contents, managing sources and inserting and formatting footnotes, endnotes, citations, and bibliographies there are workflows to streamline the steps to create this information. Notice just a few examples below, where there is a list of formal writing styles to select from, as well as a Researcher tool to find relevant information on any topic.

Formal styles supported

Researcher panel – results for 'Bill Gates'

4.1 Create and manage reference elements

This section will review steps required to create and manage reference elements.

4.1.0 Insert caption for picture or object

To be consistent about numeration and formatting use the Insert Caption tool for images and objects within Word. Note that the result is just adjacent text and is not attached.

Add a caption:

1. **Select** a picture or object
2. Select **References → Insert Caption**
3. Edit **Caption** dialog, and click **OK**
4. **Review** the results

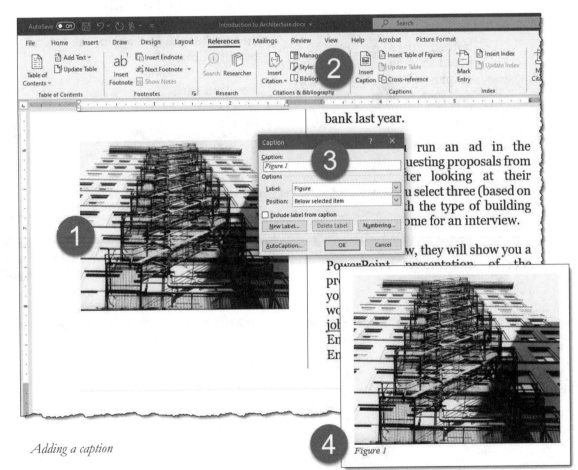

Adding a caption

4.1.1 Insert footnotes and endnotes

A footnote adds a reference at the bottom of a page, and endnote at end of document.

Insert a footnote:

5. **Click** to position cursor where a footnote reference is desired
6. Select **References → Insert Footnote**
7. Edit footnote at <u>bottom of page</u>; cursor is automatically positioned here
8. Review results at original location in document

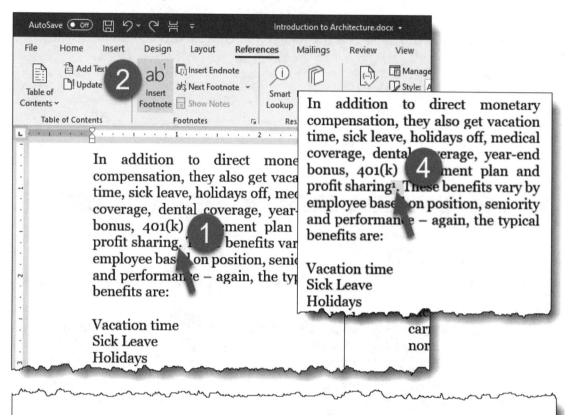

Adding a footnote reference

Insert an endnote:

1. **Click** to position cursor where endnote reference is desired
2. Select **References → Insert Endnote**
3. Edit endnote at <u>end of document</u>; cursor is automatically positioned here
4. Review results at original location in document

> During creation, to quickly jump back to the original footnote or endnote reference within document, double-click the reference number.

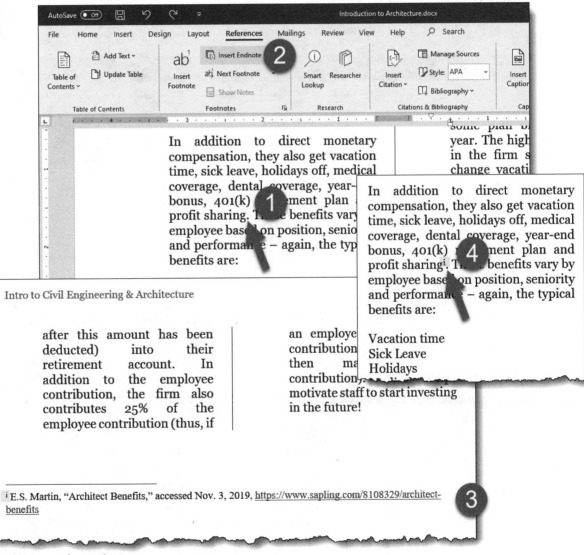

Adding an endnote reference

> Right-click on footnote or endnote to access an option to convert from footnote to endnote, or vice versa.

4.1.2 Modify footnote and endnote properties

Learn to modify the formatting properties for footnotes and endnotes.

Modify footnote or endnote properties:

1. **Click** within a footnote or endnote
2. Select **References** → **Footnote & Endnote** dialog launcher
3. Edit properties in Footnote & Endnote dialog

> Properties are either for footnotes or endnotes, depending on which was selected when the dialog was opened.

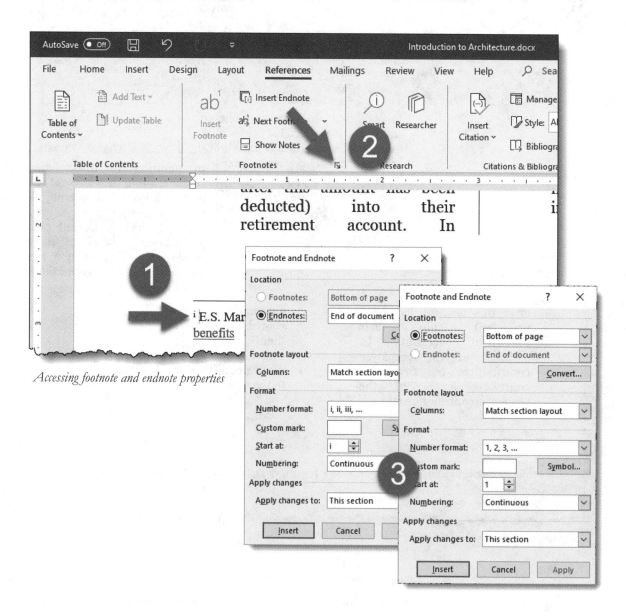

Accessing footnote and endnote properties

4.1.3 Create and modify bibliography citation sources

Know how to create and modify bibliography citations.

Create bibliography citations:

1. Select **References → Manage Sources**
2. Click the **New...** button
3. Enter the source information in the Create Source dialog
4. For the Author name, click the **Edit...** button and use the Edit Name dialog

> In the Source Manager dialog, select a source on the left and then click the **Edit...** button to edit a source.

Creating a bibliography source

A source only appears in the Source Manager dialog until inserted in the document.

4.1.4 Insert citations for bibliographies

Understand how to insert bibliography citations.

Insert bibliography citation: 🎥

1. **Click** to position cursor where citation is desired
2. Select **References → Insert Citation → pick a citation**
3. Review the results

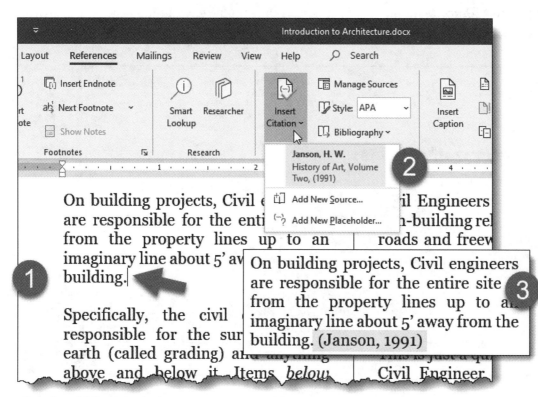

Inserting a bibliography citation

Click directly on the citation to reveal a down-arrow, which opens a menu with related commands when clicked; see image to the right.

> Notice, in the image above, the option to Add a new **Placeholder citation** as well; enter text used to recall what citation to create later.

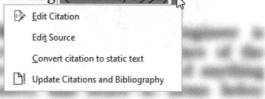

Modify an inserted bibliography citation

4.2 Create and manage reference tables

Review the steps required to insert a reference table, such as Table of Contents and Bibliography.

4.2.0 Types of reference tables

The following list of tables, which are tools found on the References tab, represent additional automation for formal documents, such as books and reports. These 'smart' tables are automatically created and updated with a click of a button.

Table of authorities

Adds a list of rules, statutes, cases, and other authorities marked in your document. This feature works in conjunction with the **Mark Citation** tool.

Table of contents

Creates a table of contents often found at the beginning of a book or report. This feature works in conjunction with specific **Styles** applied and the **Add Text** tool.

Table of figures

Inserts a table of figures used to index figures, graphs, and tables within a document. This feature works in conjunction with **Insert Caption** tool.

Bibliography

Creates a list of works cited within your document. This feature works in conjunction with **Insert Citation**, **Manage Sources**, and the selected **Style**.

Index

Adds an index, often found at the end of a book or report, which is used to locate important words or concepts. This feature works in conjunction with **Mark Entry**.

4.2.1 Insert tables of contents

A table of contents lists the page number on which a new section or chapter can be found. The automatic table of contents use the Heading styles to form the list. In the first image below, the selected text is set to Heading 1. Keep this example in mind for the following steps which outline the insertion of a table of contents.

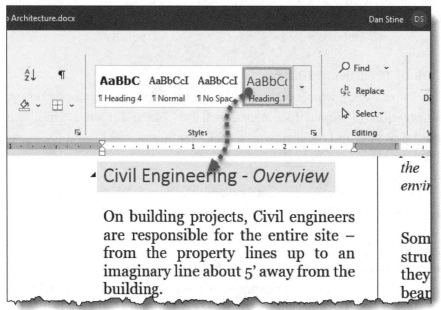

Setting text style

Insert table of contents:

1. With the cursor positioned at the desired location, click **References → Table of Contents → select an option**; e.g. Automatic Table 2
2. Review the results (see next page)

Notice, the entry "Civil Engineering – *Overview*" occurs because it was formatted as Style "Heading 1" as described previously. If the document changes, use the **References → Update Table** command; see image to right.

Table update options

Selecting a table of contents style

Table of Contents

INTRODUCTION *just the basics*

Architecture: it's where we live, shop, work and learn! This book is meant to

Reviewing the results of the new table of contents

4.2.2 Customize tables of contents

Learn to customize table of contents.

Customize table of contents:

1. Select **References → Table of Contents → Custom Table of Contents…**
2. Modify the Table of Contents dialog and sub-dialogs
3. Review results

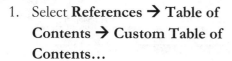

Custom Table of Contents command

Modify table of contents

4.2.3 Insert bibliographies

Understand how to insert a bibliography of cited works.

Insert bibliography:

1. Place cursor at desired location within document, then select
   References → Bibliography → pick an option
2. Review the results

All citations placed in the document are listed here. The format follows the writing Style standard selected, e.g. APA in this case. Writing and format standards help publishing and news organizations to be consistent in things like formatting, hyphenation and, for example, whether to use the Oxford Comma or not.

Placing bibliography for cited works

4.3 Practice tasks

Try the topics covered in this chapter to make sure you understand the concepts. These tasks are sequential and should be completed in the same Word document unless noted otherwise. Saving the results is optional, unless assigned by an instructor.

First Step:

✓ Open provided document **Introduction to Architecture.docx**

Task 1.1:

✓ After the word "Architecture" in the first paragraph, add a Footnote with the text "Built structures to protect people from the elements."

Task 1.2

✓ On the second page, after the first paragraph, add an Endnote with the text "The exact distance can vary."

Task 1.3

✓ Modify the Endnote format, making the number format lowercase letters.

Task 1.4:

✓ Create a bibliography source, using the same example from this chapter: History of Art, Volume Two.

Task 1.5:

✓ Insert the newly created bibliography citation at the end of the third paragraph, on the first page.

4.4 Self-exam & review questions

Self-Exam:

The following questions can be used to check your knowledge of this chapter. The answers can be found at the bottom of the next page.

1. Using Word's image/object caption tool aids in numeration and format consistency within a document. (T/F)
2. Endnotes are added at the end of a document. (T/F)
3. Word has a Manage Sources tool for citations. (T/F)
4. Ribbon tab Insert Table of Contents tool is found? _____ .
5. Word has tools to automatically manage a book's table of contents and index. (T/F)

Review Questions:

The following questions may be assigned by your instructor to assess your knowledge of this chapter. Your instructor has the answers to the review questions.

1. Footnotes are added at the end of the document. (T/F)
2. The Footnotes and Endnote dialog is accessed from the ribbon's References tab. (T/F)
3. The Insert Citation tool lists items previously added in Manage Sources. (T/F)
4. A Bibliography is a list of rules, statutes, etc. (T/F)
5. By default, the Table of Contents are defined by Heading styles. (T/F)
6. Customizing the Table of Contents is not supported. (T/F)
7. Use the following command to make the Table of Contents current if the document has changed: _____ .
8. Word allows Placeholder citations to be added, which can be completed later. (T/F)
9. Which is specifically not a Type of Source: Book, Magazine, Report? _____
10. The Styles selection, on the References tab, help enforce writing style and formatting standards. (T/F)

SELF-EXAM ANSWERS:
1 – T, **2** – T, 3 – T, **4** – References, **5** – T

Notes:

5 Insert and Format Graphic Elements

5.0 Types of graphic elements

This section starts with a high-level introduction to the features covered in this chapter.

5.0.0 An overview of graphic elements and when to use them

Word offers many graphical elements on the Insert tab. The following list is a brief introduction of what they are and when to use them.

Picture   *used to include a photograph*

Inserts raster image (e.g. a **jpg** or **png** file), which could be computer generated or a photograph. Word also provides access to an online library of stock images. When selected, use the **Picture Format** tab to edit size, artistic effects, transparency, and more.

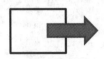

Shapes   *used to stylize the document or graphically define a sidebar*

Create ready-made shapes such as circles, squares, lines and more. When selected, use the **Shape Format** tab to modify size, color and more.

Icons   *used to visually group ideas or sections of information*

Places a highly stylized graphic used to visually communicate using symbols. When selected, use the **Graphics Format** tab to modify size, color, and more.

3D Models   *used to create interactive documents and reduce number of static pictures*

Inserts a 3D model which can be viewed from any angle by clicking and dragging the cursor over the object. When selected, use the **3D Model** tab to modify size, view, and more.

SmartArt   *manage complex graphics consisting of multiple interconnected shapes*

SmartArt are intelligent interconnected graphics used to describe workflows, processes, and more. When selected, use the **SmartArt Design** and **Format** tabs to modify styles, layouts, graphics, and more.

Chart   *used to convey data graphically*

Inserts a bar, area, or line chart to graphically display data. When selected, use the **Chart Styles** and **Format** tabs to modify styles, data, and more.

Screenshot   *used to capture information on the computer screen*

This tool is used to capture graphics currently displayed on the screen. The result is a picture element.

5.1 Insert illustrations and text boxes

Know how to place graphical elements and text boxes for the associate certification exam.

5.1.0 Insert Icons
Word offers many highly stylized icons which can be used to represent ideas graphically.

Insert Icons:

1. Click to position cursor
2. Select **Insert → Icons**
3. In the dialog, **select** an icon and click **Insert**
    a. Use search to help find desired graphics more quickly
    b. Notice the other tabs at the top of the dialog: Cutout people, etc.
4. Review results
    a. In this example, the icon was resized and had **text wrapping** changed to **In front of text**, and then repositioned to the left margin.

Inserting an icon

5.1.1 Insert shapes

Word offers many shapes to enhance graphical communication with your audience.

Insert shapes: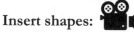

5. **Insert → Shapes → Select a shape**; e.g. Star: 5 Points
6. In desired location, click and drag diagonally to define shape size
    a. Hold down the Shift key to lock proportions while dragging
7. Review results

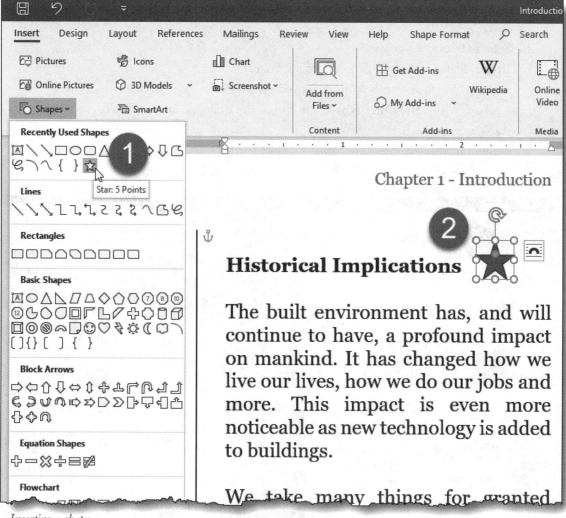

Inserting a shape

Once the shape is placed, the element is selected. Note the following options while the element is selected:

Rotation: Click and drag the rotation-icon to adjust the shape angle

Stretch: click and drag one of the edge-grips to distort the shape

Manipulate: Click and drag the gold-grip to resize the shape internally

Layout Options: Click the layout options icon to open the menu, then select an option

Tip: Holding the Shift key does the following: snaps to rotation increments *and* locks the proportions when dragging a corner grip.

Change a shape: Select a shape and click **Shape Format** (tab) → **Edit Shape** → **Change Shape**. Select a new option from the list.

Finally, the **Shape Format** tab has many additional options to modify the selected shape. Knowing how to modify a shape can save time during the exam, compared to deleting an element and starting over.

Change a shape

5.1.2 Insert pictures

Review the steps required to place an image file within the current document.

Insert Pictures:

1. Click to place cursor at desired location for image
2. **Insert → Pictures → Select an image**
3. Browse for a supported image file: e.g. jpg or png file format
4. Review the results

See the previous section on Shapes for tips on modifying the selected element: size, proportions, rotation and layout options.

Placing an image

5.1.3 Insert 3D models

Know how to place and adjust a 3D model within a document.

Insert 3D Models:

1. Click to place cursor at desired location for the 3D Model
2. **Insert → 3D Models** from online sources
3. Browse for a 3D model to insert and click **Insert**

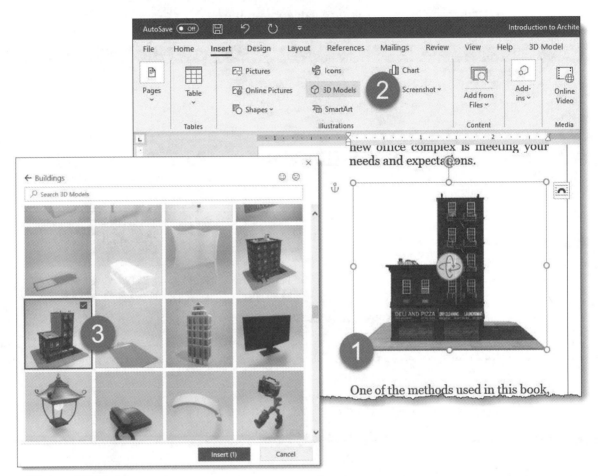

Placing a 3D Model

Adjusting the 3D Model view can be achieved in the following ways:

- Click and drag the **orbit icon** in the center of the graphic when the element is selected.

- Select the 3D Model, then click one of the preset views listed on the 3D Model tab, on the ribbon.

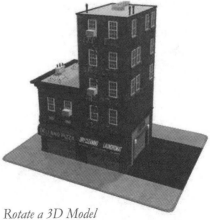

Rotate a 3D Model

5.1.4 Insert SmartArt graphics

Review how to create and manage the interconnected shapes known as SmartArt.

Insert SmartArt:

1. Click to place cursor at desired location for the SmartArt
2. **Insert → SmartArt**
3. Select an option and click **Insert**
    a. Filter the list by selecting a category on the left

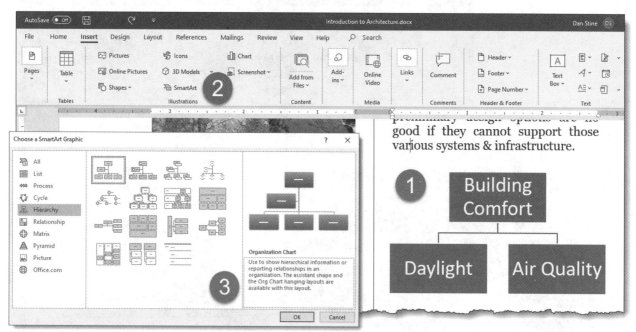

Place a SmartArt element

Use the dialog shown below to edit and arrange SmartArt. First select the element and then click the arrow on the left to reveal the organizational chart dialog.

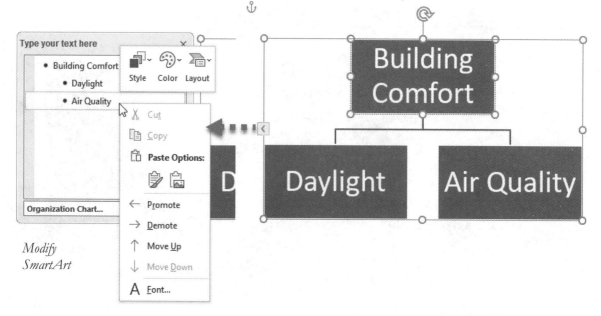

Modify SmartArt

5.1.5 Insert screenshots and screen clippings

The steps to insert a representation of current content on your screen is covered here.

Insert Screenshot:

Insert the full view of another application currently open at the cursor location.

1. Click to place cursor at desired location for the screenshot
2. **Insert → Screenshot**; select from available window previews
   a. Available Windows are based on all open applications on-screen currently

Insert screenshot

Insert Screen Clipping:

Insert a selected area of the current screen graphics at the cursor location.

1. Click to place cursor at desired location for the screen clipping
2. **Insert → Screenshot → Screen Clipping**
3. On your computer screen(s), click and draw to select an area to capture

The area highlighted is now placed in the document as a static image. Use Word's image crop tool to further refine the clipped area (which results in a smaller area).

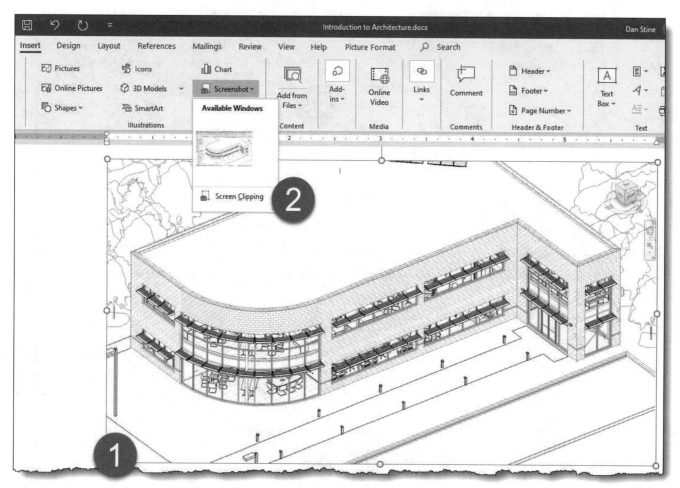

Insert screen clipping

5.1.6 Insert text boxes

Be sure to know how to place a text box, used to contain and manage specific text.

Insert text box:

1. Click to place cursor at desired location for the text box
2. **Insert → Text Box → Select an option**
3. Modify and populate the text box
   a. Use the grips and layout options like steps previously described for shapes
   b. Click within text box to type text

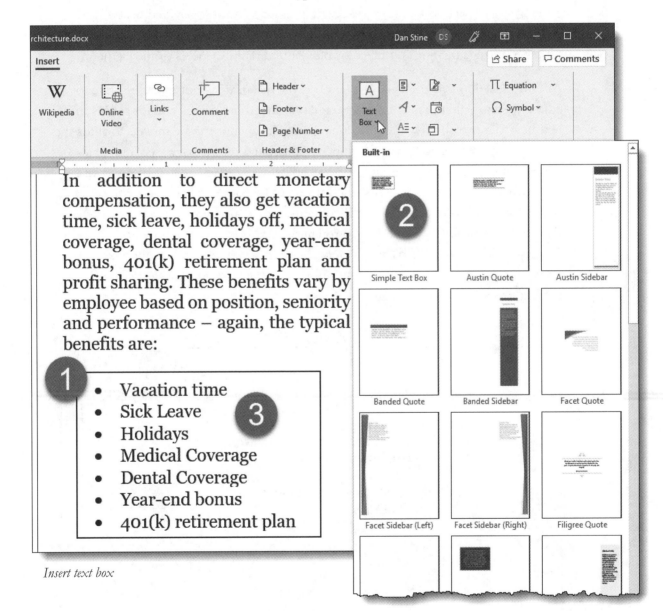

Insert text box

5.2 Format illustrations and text boxes

This section covers formatting images and text boxes.

5.2.0 Format text boxes

The previous section provided instruction on placing a text box within the current document. Once placed, there are several formatting options available.

Selecting the edge of a section box reveals several in-canvas controls covered below. The **Shape Format** tab is also visible on the Ribbon, when the text box is selected, which contains tools to change the line and fill color plus other graphic aspects of the element.

A. **Anchor:** Used to control when the text box moves, or does not move, relative to adjacent edits. Additional lines and paragraphs added before the anchor causes the text box to move down within the document. The anchor can be moved towards the top of the current page to keep it properly positioned on the page (see item D also).

B. **Grips:** Dragging a corner or edge grip will adjust the size of the text box and adjust the text within. Warning: it is possible for text to be completely hidden if the text box is too small relative to the text it contains. Not available for in-line with text.

C. **Rotation Control:** Click and drag to rotate the text box and its contents.

D. **Layout Options:** Click the layout options icon to review the in-line and text wrapping options. Selecting 'Fix position on page' will prevent any edits from moving the text box on the page.

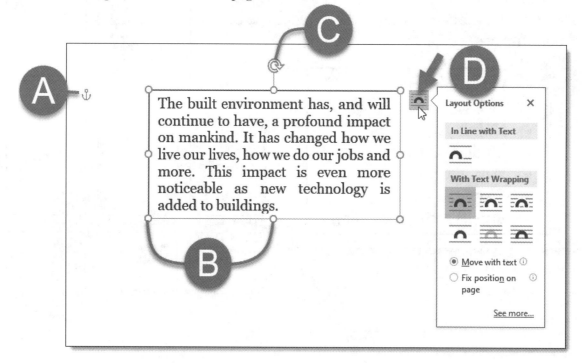

5.2.1 Apply artistic effects

Apply a non-destructive artistic effect to an image file, which may be undone later.

Apply artistic effect:

1. Select the image you wish to enhance with an artistic effect
2. Click **Picture Format → Artistic Effects → Select an option**; e.g. Pencil Sketch

Notice each effect has a name, which appears in a tooltip as shown in the image below.

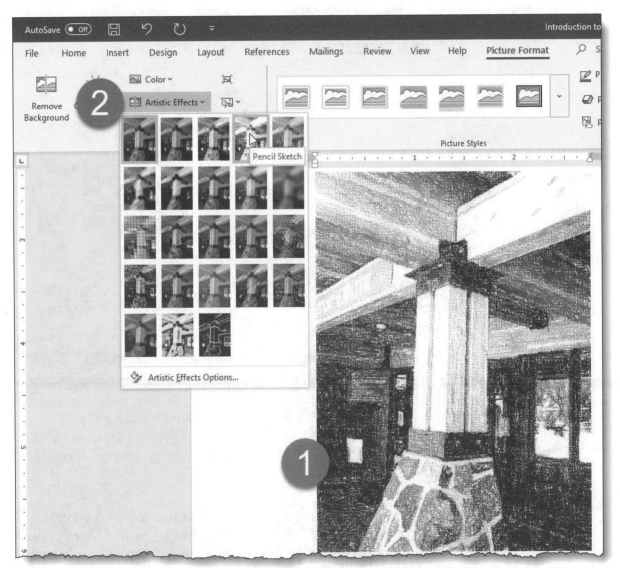

Applying an artistic effect to an image

5.2.2 Apply picture effects and picture styles

Learn how to apply a picture effect and picture style to a selected image. Know the terms.

Apply Picture Effect:

1. Select the image you wish to enhance with a picture effect
2. Click **Picture Format** → **Picture Effects** → **Select an option**; e.g. Preset 9

> Notice each effect has a name, which appears in a tooltip as shown in the image below.

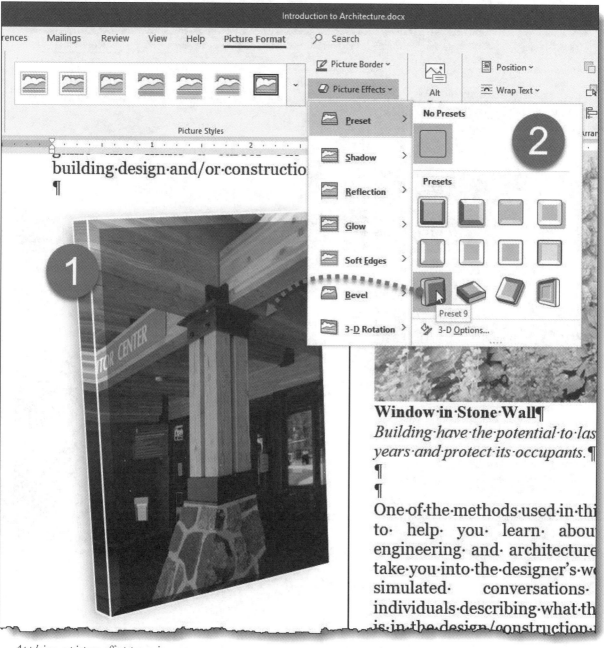

Applying a picture effect to an image

Apply Picture Style:

1. Select the image you wish to enhance with a picture style
2. Click **Picture Format → Picture Style → Select an option**; e.g. Soft Edge Oval

> Notice each style has a name, which appears in a tooltip

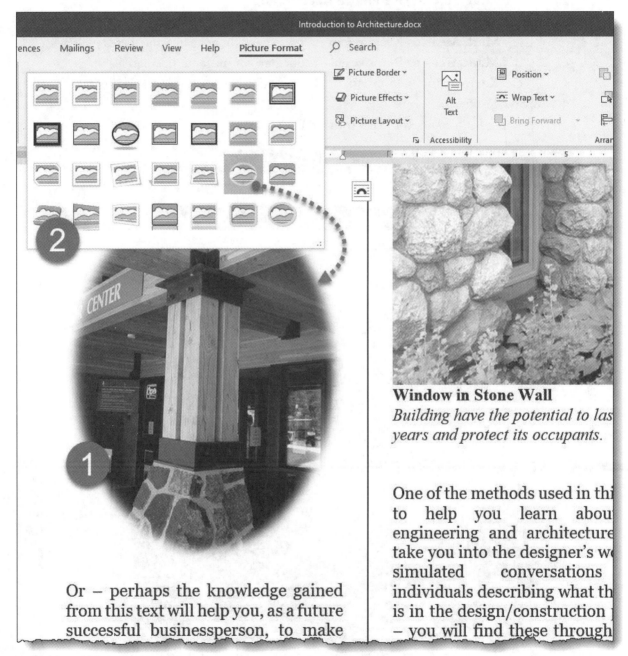

Applying a picture style to an image

5.2.3 Remove picture backgrounds

Use this option to remove a portion of the image, exposing the area behind the image.

Remove Picture Background: 🎥

1. Select the image you wish to remove background from
2. Click **Picture Format → Remove Background**
3. Magenta fill defines area to remove; do the following:
    a. **Mark Areas to Keep**: remove a portion of the magenta filled area
    b. **Mark Areas to Remove**: add to the current magenta filled area
    c. **Keep Changes to finish**; or Discard All Changes to cancel command
4. Review results
5. Optional: Set *Wrap Text* to **In Front of Text**

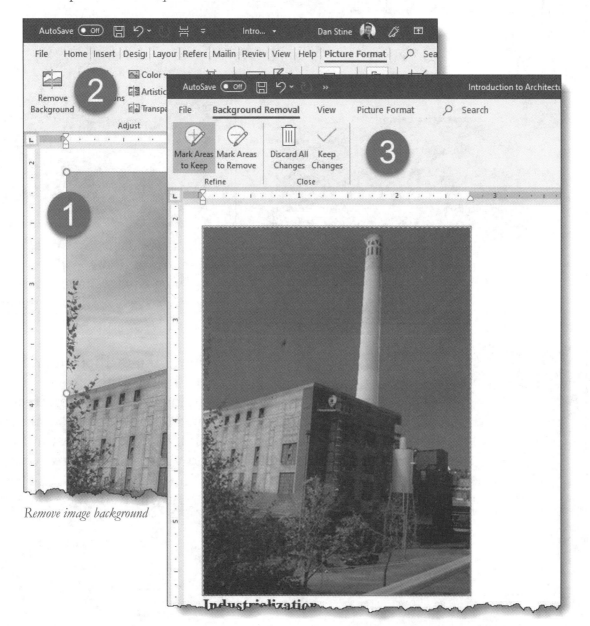

Remove image background

The image below shows the result, with the sky behind the building removed in this example. This might be done for aesthetic effect or to draw more attention to the building and smokestack.

To help show that the image has a transparent background, change the **Wrap Text** to Square or In Front of Text for example. When moved over text or another image the content beneath the modified image can be seen, as shown in step #5 below.

Resultant image with background removed (#4), plus options 'wrap text' setting (#5)

Later, the image background may be restored by selecting the image, clicking Remove Background and click Discard All Changes. Thus, the Remove Image is non-destructive to the original content loaded in the current document.

5.2.4 Format graphic elements

Word supports a multitude of formatting functionality for graphics elements; here are several.

Format graphic elements:

1. Select the image you wish to modify
2. Click the **Picture Format** tab on the Ribbon

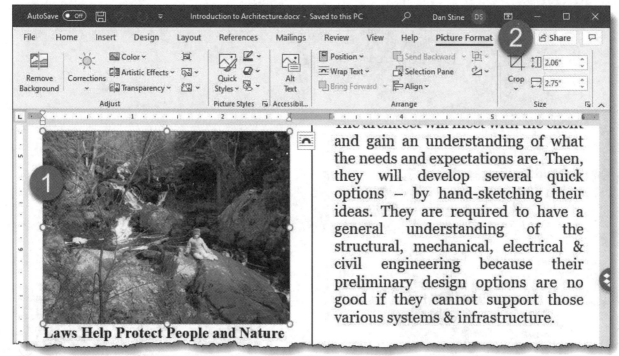

Format graphic element options

With the graphic element selected, the following options are available:

- **Adjust:** Corrections (e.g. brighten, sharpen), Color adjust, Transparency

- **Picture Styles:** Border, Effects (e.g. shadows, reflection, 3d), Layout

- **Accessibility:** Alt Text (for the visually impaired)

- **Arrange:** Position, Wrap Text, Align, Group, Rotate

- **Size:** Crop, Width, Height plus advanced options via dialog box launcher shown to the right.

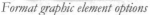

5.2.5 Format SmartArt graphics

Review the ways in which SmartArt might be formatted.

Format SmartArt graphics:

1. Select the SmartArt graphic you wish to modify
2. Click **Format** on the Ribbon
3. Select the text or graphic to modify

Format SmartArt graphics

With the text selected, in the SmartArt text dialog, the following options are possible:

- **WordArt Styles:** Styles, Text Fill, Text Outline, Text Effects

With a SmartArt, or sub-component selected, the following options are possible:

- **Shape Styles:** Styles, Shape Fill, Shape Outline, Shape Effects
- **Accessibility:** Alt Text (for the visually impaired)
- **Arrange:** Position, Wrap Text, Align, Group, Rotate
- **Size:** Width, and Height

> Shape styles, effects, etc. have names (hover to see via tooltip). Be sure to look for the correct name when provided in the exam.

5.2.6 Format 3D models

Once placed, 3D Models have several formatting options available.

Format 3D Models:

1. Select the 3D Model you wish to modify
2. Click **3D Model** on the Ribbon

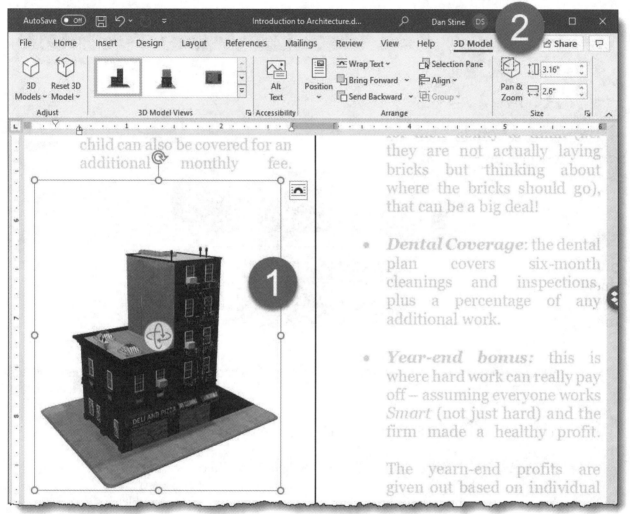

Format 3D Models

With the 3D Model selected, the following options are available:

- **Adjust:** Select a new 3D model or reset
- **3D Model Views:** Select a pre-defined view (e.g. front, top, etc.)
- **Accessibility:** Alt Text (for the visually impaired)
- **Arrange:** Position, Wrap Text, Align, Group, Rotate
- **Size:** Pan and Zoom, Crop, Width, Height

5.3 Add text to graphic elements

Graphic elements allow text to be placed in more specific locations within a document.

5.3.0 Selecting graphic elements

Selecting elements usually just requires a direct click with the cursor positioned over the desired items. However, some elements like SmartArt and charts, have sub-elements which may be selected with a second click. For the SmartArt example shown below, a third click was required to access the text, for editing. Holding the Ctrl key allows multiple elements to be selected, or unselected – as long as the elements are not set to in-line with text.

5.3.1 Add and modify text in text boxes

Understand how to add text to a text box, and then modify it.

Add and modify text in text boxes:

1. Click within text box and enter text or select text
2. Use the temporary text formatting tool to modify text

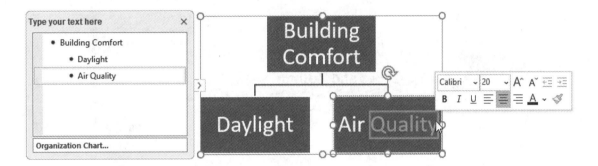

Add and modify text in text box

All the usual text formatting work on text within a textbox.

5.3.2 Add and modify text in shapes

Know how to add and modify text within a shape.

Add and modify text in shapes:

1. Click a shape element
2. *Right-click and select* **Edit Text**

> The Edit Text command changes to Edit Text once text has been added as shown below

Add text to a shape

Similar to editing a text box, covered in the previous outcome, text within a shape can be edited just like all other text in Word.

5.3.3 Add and modify SmartArt graphic content

Review how to add and modify text within SmartArt.

Add and Modify SmartArt graphics content:

1. Select the SmartArt graphic you wish to modify
2. Click **Format** on the Ribbon
3. Modify the text within the **Type your text here** dialog

Add and Modify SmartArt contents

With the text selected, in the SmartArt text dialog, the following options are possible:

- **WordArt Styles:** Styles, Text Fill, Text Outline, Text Effects
- **Accessibility:** Alt Text (for entire element and individual components)

5.4 Modify graphic elements

Graphic elements, such as images and text boxes, can be positioned in several ways within a document. Some of these options will be covered in this section.

5.4.0 Resize graphic elements

Most graphic elements may be selected and resized by dragging the corner or edge grips on-screen. If more accuracy is required, typing in a specific height and/or width is also possible.

A. With the graphic selected, edit the width or height on the elements format tab, Picture Format example shown below.

B. For even more control, click the dialog icon on the size panel. Here, a percentage may be used to resize the image. The aspect ratio can also be unlocked, to allow the image to be distorted.

Re-size options for selected graphic

5.4.1 Position objects

Objects, like shapes, text boxes and pictures can be positioned in several ways on the page.

Position an image:

1. Select an image to position
2. Click the **Layout Options** icon and select an option

The steps are the same for shapes and text boxes

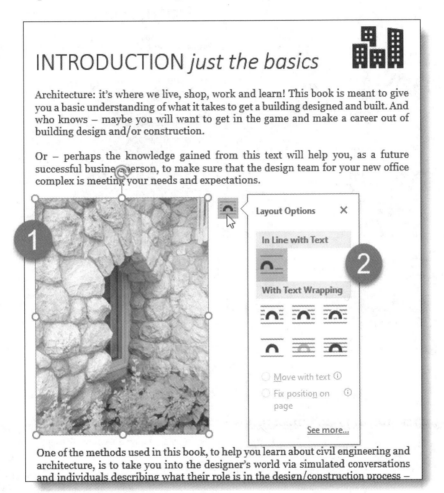

Position an image

The **In Line with Text** option is the default. In this case, think of the object as one giant letter. Notice this results in a lot of white space (i.e. blank paper) in this example.

Another popular layout option is **Square** as shown on the left side of the example below. In this case the text fills the space around the image, leaving less white space.

Selecting **Behind Text** or **In Front of Text** allows the object to be placed anywhere on the sheet without affecting the text. The example below, on the right, shows the Behind Text option. In this case the text may be too hard to read, unless the image brightness or transparency is reduced.

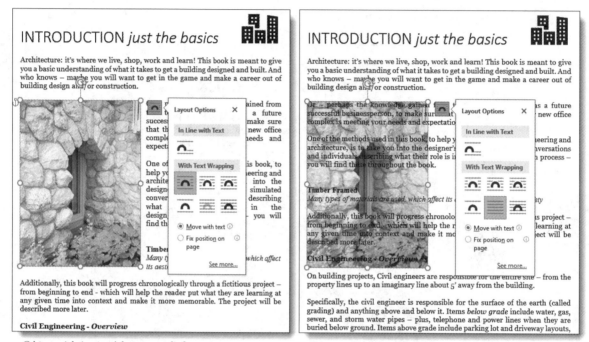

Object with 'square' layout applied   *Object with 'behind text' layout applied*

Position:

When an image is set to anything other than In Line, simply **click and drag an object** to change its position on the page.

Anchor:

When an object is selected, an **anchor icon** appears to indicate its relative position on the page; see example to the right. This icon can be repositioned to make sure it moves with the correct section. For example, moving it to the top left of the page will generally keep the object from moving while editing other aspects of the same page.

Anchor icon for selected object

5.4.2 Wrap text around objects

Like the steps just covered, text can be made to wrap around objects such as images, text boxes and shapes. For the full picture, review the previous two pages along with this section.

Wrap text around an image:

1. Select an image to modify its properties
2. Click the **Layout Options** icon and select a 'text wrapping' option

> The text automatically wraps as the object is moved around the page.

who knows – maybe you will want to get in the game and make a career out of building design and/or construction.

Or – perhaps the knowledge gained from this text will help you, as a future successful businessperson, to make sure that the design team for your new office complex is meeting your needs and expectations.

One of the methods used in this book, to help you learn about civil engineering and architecture, is to take you into the designer's world via simulated conversations and individuals describing what their role is in the design/construction process – you will find these throughout the book.

Timber Framed
Many types of materials are used, which affect its aesthetic, longevity and safety

Additionally, this book will progress chronologically through a fictitious project –

Wrap text around an object

to get in the game and make a career out of

from future e sure office s and

ok, to g and o the ulated cribing the u will

Timber Framed
Many types of materials are used, which affect its aesthetic, longevity and safety

Additionally, this book will progress chronologically through a fictitious project – from beginning to end - which will help the reader put what they are learning at

5.4.3 Add alternative text to objects for accessibility

Add audibly descriptive text to aid people with visual impairments, when using a screen reader.

Add Alt Text to an image:

1. Select an image
2. Click Picture Format → Alt Text
3. Enter text which describes the image in the Alt Text panel

> Check the **Mark as Decorative** option if the image is not a meaningful part of the document but is just meant to aesthetically embellish the page layout.

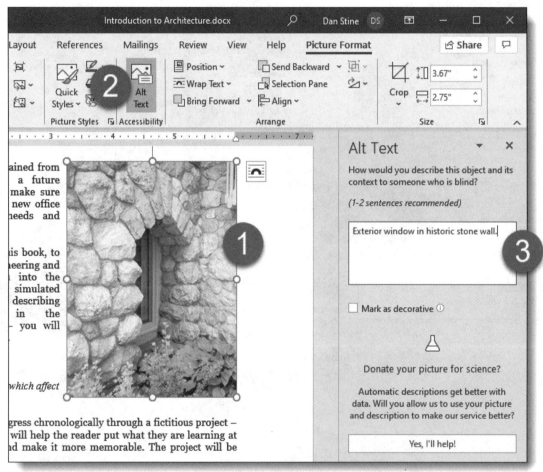

Adding Alt Text to an image

5.5 Practice tasks

Try the topics covered in this chapter to make sure you understand the concepts. These tasks are sequential and should be completed in the same Word document unless noted otherwise. Saving the results is optional, unless assigned by an instructor.

First Step:

- ✓ Open provided document **Introduction to Architecture.docx**

Task 1.1:

- ✓ On the second page, after the first paragraph in the Architecture – Overview section, add two returns (aka enter key) and **insert the provided image**: Tall Building.png.

Task 1.2

- ✓ To the new image just added, apply the **artistic effect** Pencil Grayscale.

Task 1.3

- ✓ Change the **width** of the new image to 2.25".

Task 1.4:

- ✓ For new image, change **text wrapping** to behind text.

Task 1.5:

- ✓ Add a **simple text box** to the very end of the document with the text "End of document."

5.6 Self-exam & review questions

Self-Exam:

The following questions can be used to check your knowledge of this chapter. The answers can be found at the bottom of the next page.

1. 3D models can be viewed from different angles within the document. (T/F)
2. The Screenshot tool can only capture the entire computer screen. (T/F)
3. Icons are inserted from the ribbon's Draw tab. (T/F)
4. Which icon helps control an image/object's position on a page, and is only visible when the image/object is selected? _____ .
5. To reveal the organizational chart, first select SmartArt and then click the arrow on the left. (T/F)

Review Questions:

The following questions may be assigned by your instructor to assess your knowledge of this chapter. Your instructor has the answers to the review questions.

1. Icons are used to manage complex graphics consisting of multiple interconnected shapes. (T/F)
2. When a picture or object is selected, a rotate icon is visible. (T/F)
3. Holding the Shift key while dragging a corner grip locks the proportions. (T/F)
4. The Pictures command places an image file, like png and jpg formats. (T/F)
5. Rotation of a Text Box is not possible. (T/F)
6. An image must be selected before the ribbon's Picture Format tab is visible. (T/F)
7. What ribbon tab is the Screen Clipping tool found on? _____ .
8. It is not possible to add text to a Shape, such as an oval. (T/F)
9. Feature used for images/objects, to aid people with visual impairments ____ _____ .
10. The Width and/or Height may be modified via the Picture Format tab. (T/F)

6 Manage Document Collaboration

Introduction

In this chapter you will review a few ways in which multiple people might work together on the same document. This includes managing comments and change tracking.

6.0 Collaborating with a team

When a document needs to be authored and/or edited by multiple people, it is important to define the team workflow to prevent loss of work. This section overs this concept and the benefits of team collaboration.

6.0.0 Benefits of team collaboration within Word

It is often helpful to get other's input on the development of a document.

<u>Manage comments</u>

Word can manage comments which are not directly part of the formal document. This facilitates document reviews where those offering review comments are not allowed or encouraged to edit the document. This can also be used by a co-author who wants to pose a question about a passage or graphic, which keeps the comments in one place, rather than using a messaging system or email. Commands can be added throughout the document. Others can reply to the comment. Comments may be marked as resolved or deleted.

<u>Track changes</u>

Word can also track changes for multiple document editors. This system tracks text, graphics, and punctuation changes. The deleted or replaced content is struck out and maintained in-line in the document to compare the new content with the old. In the end, tracked changed are accepted or rejected.

6.0.1 Sharing a document

When a Word document is stored in OneDrive, Microsoft's cloud storage system, or within Microsoft Teams, it is possible to share the document and facilitate multiple people to review and/or edit at the same time.

To share a document stored in OneDrive, click the **Share** button in the upper right (see image).

6.1 Add and manage comments

The certification exam requires knowledge of adding and managing comments in a document.

6.1.0 When to add comments

Comments can be added by a document's sole author to makes 'notes to self'. They may also be added by co-authors and/or editors to track a multitude of information. For example, suggestions to re-word a section for clarity, or to suggest a reference be added, and more. In general, it is better to leave a comment if there is a chance the document might be improved, rather than lose the thought and the opportunity to improve the document's accuracy, clarity or intent.

6.1.1 Add comments

Know how to add a comment to the document, which does not affect the current layout or formatting.

Add a comment:

1. Place the cursor or select text at the location to add a comment
2. Click **Review → New Comment**
   a. Note that **Show Comments** is toggled on by default
3. Type a comment in the comment box; e.g. "Cite examples for this statement"

Adding a comment

6.1.2 Review and reply to comments

Understand how to see each comment and reply to them when needed.

Review a comment:

Existing comments can be made visible, if not already, and then reviewed one at a time.

1. *If not already toggled on*, Click **Review → Show Comments**
   a. Note: **Simple Markup** must be selected in the adjacent *Tracking* panel
2. Click **Next**, or **Previous**, to cycle through all comments in the current document

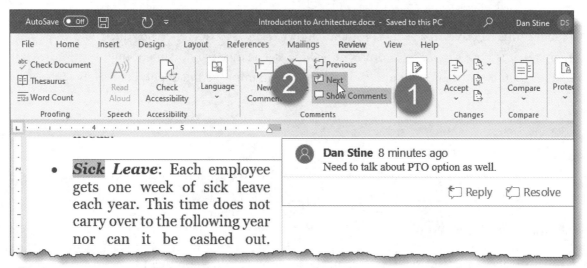

Review comments

Reply to a comment:

It is possible to reply to a comment, perhaps to request more information or to disagree. When another user replies, their name will appear next to the comment; this is based on the Word account settings.

1. In a comment, click **Reply**
2. Enter the desired reply

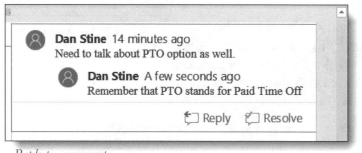

Reply to a comment

6.1.3 Resolve comments

When a comment has been implemented in the document, set it to resolved.

Resolve a comment:

1. *If not already toggled on,* Click **Review** → **Show Comments**
   a. Note: **Simple Markup** must be selected in the adjacent *Tracking* panel
2. Click **Resolve** for a comment

Notice the comment is not deleted and may be **Reopened** if needed.

Resolve a comment

When **Show Comments** is not toggled on, a non-printing symbol appears where a comment is within the document as shown in the example below. Clicking this symbol will temporarily show the comment without turning on all comments. Note that the visibility of comments is also tied to the **Display for Review** drop-down option in the Tracking panel.

Many of the people in the construction industry work 40+ hours per week. Their compensation is often based on *Salary* rather than *Hourly*; this means they will get the exact same amount in their paycheck

Comment indicator icon

6.1.4 Delete comments

When a comment is no longer needed, it may be deleted.

Delete a comment: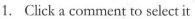

1. Click a comment to select it
2. Select **Review → Delete → Delete**
   a. Or **Delete All Comments in Document**

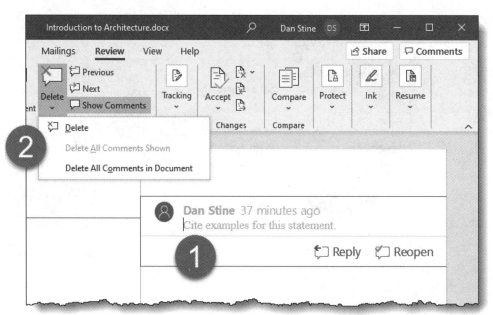

Delete a comment

6.2 Manage change tracking

The certification exam requires an understanding of managing changes in a document such that others know what changed and by whom.

6.2.0 When to use track changes

When a co-author is not entirely sure about an addition or modification to a document, it is best to use track changes so others have a chance to review and approve. This can be especially important in contracts and legal documents, to ensure everyone is aware of all elements of the document. This feature can also be helpful to use when developing a report for a group project in school.

6.2.1 Track changes

Once Track Changes is toggled on, any modifications to the document are tracked. This also means that nothing can be permanently deleted.

Toggle on Track changes:

Before making any changes to be tracked, the feature must be toggled on.

1. Select **Review → Track Changes → Track Changes**
2. While Track Changes is toggled on, the tool on the Ribbon is highlighted as shown here.

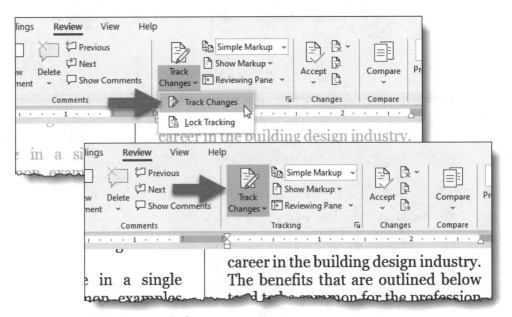

Turning on track changes

Tracked Change Example:

With track changes toggled on, changes can be made to the document.

1. Make a change to the document; e.g. delete the word "even"
2. Notice the vertical red line indicating the location of a change

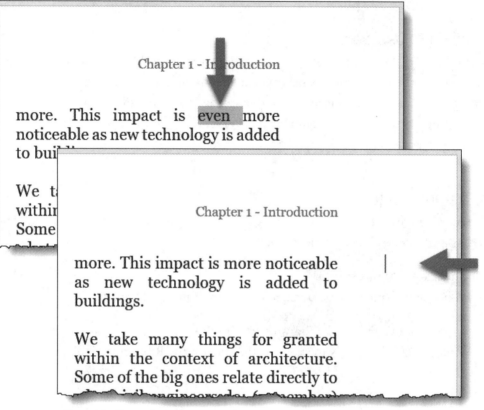

Example of a tracked change

6.2.2 Review tracked changes

Anyone working in a document with tracked changes may review the changes made.

Review tracked changes:

1. Select **Review → Display for Review** (drop-down) **→ All Markup**
2. Review changes; e.g. the word "even" has been deleted (red text with strikeout line)

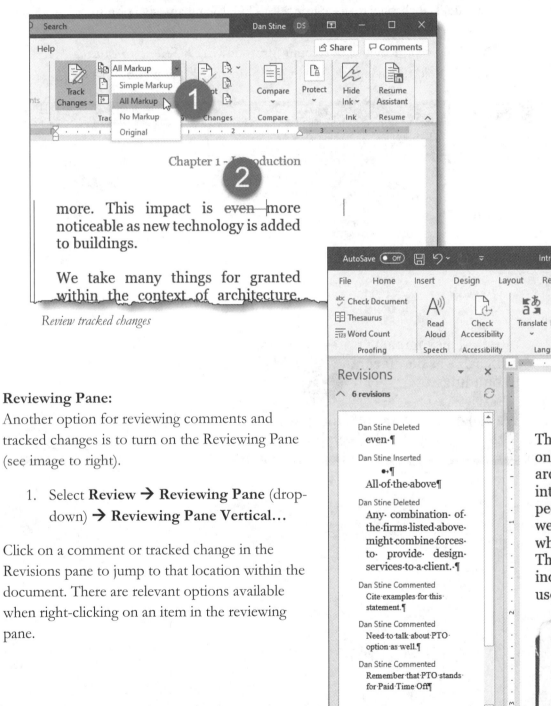

Review tracked changes

Reviewing Pane:

Another option for reviewing comments and tracked changes is to turn on the Reviewing Pane (see image to right).

1. Select **Review → Reviewing Pane** (drop-down) **→ Reviewing Pane Vertical…**

Click on a comment or tracked change in the Revisions pane to jump to that location within the document. There are relevant options available when right-clicking on an item in the reviewing pane.

Reviewing Pane

6.2.3 Accept and reject tracked changes

Later, after changes are made, when Track Changes is enabled, it is possible to accept or reject those changes. Accept makes the change permanent and reject is like an undo for a change.

Accept or reject tracked changes:

1. Select a tracked change, to accept or reject, by clicking anywhere on it
2. Click one of the following:
    a. To accept: **Review** → **Accept** (drop-down) → *Select an option*
    b. To Reject: **Review** → **Reject** (drop-down) → *Select an option*

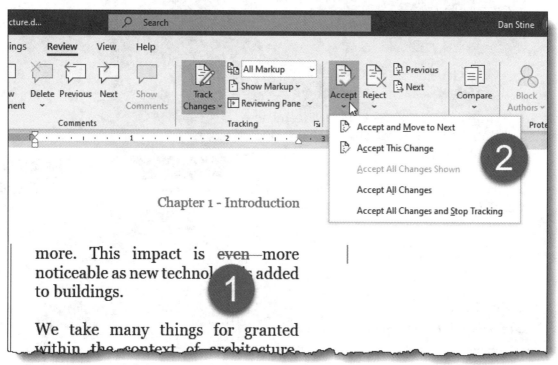

Accept or reject a tracked change

6.2.4 Lock and unlock change tracking 🎥

To help prevent others from turning off track changes, it is possible to lock the feature on using a password.

Lock change tracking:

1. Select **Review** → **Track Changes** → **Lock Tracking**
2. Enter a Password, and then re-enter the Password to confirm

Lock change tracking

Unlock change tracking:

1. Select **Review** → **Track Changes** → **Lock Tracking**
2. Enter the Password

6.3 Practice tasks

Try the topics covered in this chapter to make sure you understand the concepts. These tasks are sequential and should be completed in the same Word document unless noted otherwise. Saving the results is optional, unless assigned by an instructor.

First Step:

- ✓ Open provided document **Introduction to Architecture.docx**

Task 1.1:

- ✓ Select the entire first paragraph and **add comment** "Consider text effect for first paragraph."

Task 1.2

- ✓ **Reply** to comment on page 7 with the following text: "Task completed."

Task 1.3

- ✓ **Resolve** the task on page 8.

Task 1.4:

- ✓ Enable **Track Changes** in the document.

Task 1.5:

- ✓ Create a tracked change: delete the description of Dental Coverage on page 9.

6.4 Self-exam & review questions

Self-Exam:

The following questions can be used to check your knowledge of this chapter. The answers can be found at the bottom of the next page.

1. Multiple people can work in the same document, at the same time, when it is saved on OneDrive or Teams. (T/F)
2. It is possible to Reply to a comment. (T/F)
3. Comments may be deleted via the ribbon's Review tab. (T/F)
4. Turn on Reviewing Pane to easily see all revisions listed. (T/F)
5. When Track Changes is on, nothing in the document may be deleted. (T/F)

Review Questions:

The following questions may be assigned by your instructor to assess your knowledge of this chapter. Your instructor has the answers to the review questions.

1. The New Comment command is found on the ribbon's insert tab. (T/F)
2. Resolving a comment is not the same as Deleting a comment. (T/F)
3. It is not possible to delete all comments, within a document, at once. (T/F)
4. To prevent Track Changes from being turned off, use Lock Tracking. (T/F)
5. Individual Tracked Changes can be accepted and become part of the main document. (T/F)
6. As each change is considered, it is not possible to accept all Tracked Changes at once within a document. (T/F)
7. To prevent someone turning off Track Changes, the Lock Tracking requires what be provided when turning it on? _____ .
8. Rather than deleting text, Track Changes modifies replaced/modified text to the color red with a strikethrough line through it. (T/F)
9. Track Changes is used when the editor is not sure about a change, or others need to see what has changed. (T/F)
10. Comments are used as a quicker way to review and comment on a document, without the need to try and correct anything. (T/F)

Notes:

7 Practice Exam Software Overview

Introduction

This chapter will highlight the practice exam software provided with this book, including accessing the exam, installing required files, user interface and how to interpret the results. Taking this practice exam, after studying this book, will help ensure a successful result when taking the actual Microsoft Office Specialist Certified Associate exam at a test center.

The practice exam questions are similar, not identical, to the actual exam.

Important Things to Know

Here are a few big picture things you should keep in mind:

- **Practice Exam – First Steps**
    - The practice exam, that comes with this book, is taken on **your own computer**
    - You need to have **Word installed** and ready to use during the practice exam
    - You must download the practice exam software from SDC Publications
        - See inside-front cover of this book for access instructions
    - **Required Word files** for the practice exam
        - Files downloaded with practice exam software
        - The practice exam software opens the files when they are needed
    - Note which questions you got wrong, and study those topics

- **Practice Exam - Details**
    - Questions: 35
    - Timed: 50 minutes
    - Passing: 70%
    - Results: Presented upon completion

This practice exam can be taken multiple times. But it is recommended that you finish studying this book before taking the practice exam. There are only 35 questions total, so you don't want to get to a point where all the questions, and their answers, have been memorized. This will not help with the actual exam as they are not the same questions.

This practice exam can be taken multiple times.

Practice Exam Overview

The **practice exam** included with this book can be downloaded from the publisher's website using the **access code** found on the inside-front cover. This is a good way to check your skills prior to taking the official exam, as the intent is to offer similar types of questions in roughly the same format as the formal exam. This practice exam is taken at home, work or school, on your own computer. You must have Word installed to successfully answer the in-application questions.

This is a test drive for the exam process, including:

- Understanding the test software
- How to mark and return to questions
- Exam question format
- Live in-application steps
- How the results are presented at the exam conclusion

Here is a sample of what the practice exam looks like… note that Word is automatically opened and positioned directly above the practice exam user interface.

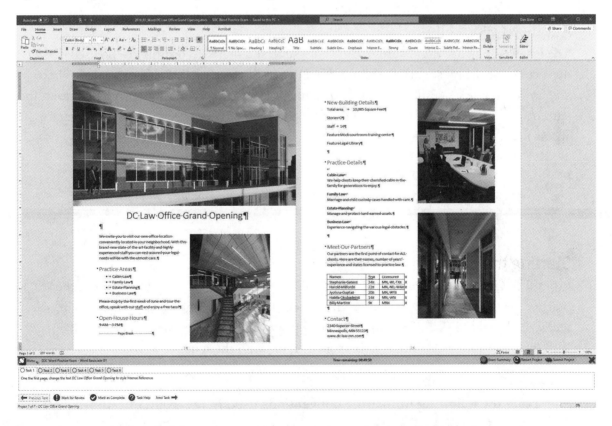

Sample question from included practice exam

Having taken the practice exam can remove some anxiety one may have going into an exam that may positively impact a career search or advancement.

Download and Install the Practice Exam

Follow the instructions on the inside-front cover of this book using the provided access code to download the practice exam. Once the ZIP file is downloaded you must extract the files into a folder that you create.

Download steps:

- Create a folder on your desktop or C drive, such as **C:\MOS Installer**
- Double-click on the downloaded ZIP file
- Copy all the folders/files from the ZIP file to the newly created folder

To install the practice Exam software on your PC-based computer simply double-click the Setup.exe file in the newly created folder. Follow the prompts on screen to complete the installation. Once complete, the folder you just created, and its contents, may be deleted.

Required Word Files

The installed practice exam software includes several required Word files to be used during the exam. For the most part, the software will open the files when they are needed. There are, however, a few questions that require a file be selected and imported. In those cases, the current working folder is changed so the file should be directly accessible when trying to access it.

For the practice exam, the required files are installed automatically.

Starting the Exam

From the Windows Start menu, click the **SDC Word Practice Exam** icon to start the practice exam. If you have purchased and installed more than one SDC practice exam, select the desired practice exam from the list that appears. At this point, the practice exam opens with the timer running. Word is also opened, along with the required workbook.

> **Note the following formatting conventions used in the exam questions:**
> - **Bold text** is used to indicate file or folder names as well as setting names.
> - Clicking on underlined text copies it to the clipboard. Use **Ctrl + V** to paste into Word to avoid typing errors.
> - Text in "quotation marks" represents existing text within the document.

Practice Exam User Interface (UI)

The following image, and subsequent list, highlight the features of the practice exam's user interface.

User Interface details:

- **Menu:** (drop-down list)
    - **About** – Exam software version information
    - **Float Application Window** – Use to reposition practice exam on the desktop
    - **Dock to Desktop Bottom** – Default option, exam fixed to bottom of screen
    - **Show Status Bar** – Toggle visibility at bottom of screen
    - **Exam Summary** – Review marked questions
    - **Finish Exam** – Grade the exam
    - **Close** – Closes the Practice Exam and Word
- **Task Tabs:** Each tab contains a question for the current project and may be marked for review or as completed. Click a tab to view its question or use Previous/Next buttons.
- **Time Remaining:** Time remaining for the 50 minute timed exam
- **Exam Summary:** Review marked questions and return to previous project/question
- **Project Controls:**
    - **Restart Project** – Discards all changes made to the current workbook
    - **Submit Project** – Advance to next project or exam completion on last project
- **Close App:** Closes the Practice Exam and Word
- **Current Project:** Current project name and number listed for reference on status bar
- **Task Controls:** *for the current project...*
    - **Previous Task** – View the previous task/question

- o **Mark for Review** – *Optional:* When unsure of the answer, mark task for review
- o **Mark as Complete** – *Optional:* When confident, mark the task as complete
- o **Task Help** – *Optional:* Reveal steps required to achieve a correct answer
- o **Next Task** – Advance to the next task/question

When unsure of the correct answer, after multiple attempts, click the **Task Help** button to reveal the steps required to answer the current question. The image below shows an example.

Practice exam - Help example

The following image shows an example of tasks marked for review and as complete. This is optional, and just meant as a way of tracking one's progress. It is possible to advance to the next project without marking any tasks.

Practice exam – Marked task exams

Practice Exam Results

When you complete the practice exam, you will find out if you passed or failed. Be sure to note which questions were answered incorrectly and review those related sections in the book.

Conclusion

As with any formal exam, the more you practice the more likely you are to have successful results. So, be sure to take the time to download the provided practice exam and give it a try before you head off to the testing facility and take the actual exam.

Good luck!

Microsoft Word Introduction and Certification Study Guide
Exam Day Study Guide

Remembering where the right tools and commands are is half the battle. Leading up to exam day, use this handy reference sheet to firm up your knowledge of important topics that will help you pass the Word exam.

Reminders

- ✓ Bring **photo ID**
- ✓ Know your Certiport **username** and **password**
- ✓ Bring exam **payment confirmation**
- ✓ Know where the testing center is; e.g. have the **building address**

Tips

- ✓ Carefully read each question
- ✓ If unsure, mark question for review and come back to it later if you have time
- ✓ Click underlined text in question to copy that text to the clipboard
- ✓ Accept all defaults unless otherwise instructed

Commands

- ⬇ **Home** tab
  - ✓ Format Painter
  - ✓ Text Effects
  - ✓ Line and Paragraph Spacing
  - ✓ Bulleted/Numbered List
  - ✓ Increase/Decrease Indent
  - ✓ Clear All Formatting
  - ✓ Styles
  - ✓ Cell Styles
  - ✓ Find/Replace & Advanced Find
- ⬇ **Insert** tab
  - ✓ Page Breaks
  - ✓ Table
  - ✓ Pictures
  - ✓ Shapes
  - ✓ 3D Models
  - ✓ SmartArt
  - ✓ Header & Footer; insert, modify, delete
  - ✓ Text Box
  - ✓ Bookmark
  - ✓ Cross-reference
  - ✓ Link
  - ✓ Symbol, special character

- ⬇ **Design** tab
  - ✓ Document Formatting Gallery (style set)
  - ✓ Watermark
  - ✓ Page Color
  - ✓ Page Border
- ⬇ **Layout** tab
  - ✓ Page Setup dialog (small icon in lower right); *Manage Headers/Footers*
  - ✓ Columns
  - ✓ Breaks; page, section & column
- ⬇ **References** tab
  - ✓ Table of Contents
  - ✓ Footnote/Endnote
  - ✓ Citations & Bibliography
- ⬇ **Review** tab
  - ✓ Comments
  - ✓ Track Changes
- ⬇ **View** tab
  - ✓ Freeze Panes; *Top Row, First Column*
- ⬇ **File** tab
  - ✓ Save As, Alternate file formats
  - ✓ Info, Properties, Check for issues
  - ✓ Print, Print settings
  - ✓ Share

Notes:

Index

SDC PUBLICATIONS **True or False: Word supports a custom page size.**	Find, Home (tab)
SDC PUBLICATIONS **What is added, by default, between columns?**	Go To
SDC PUBLICATIONS **Applying a Style Set can change the look of which part of a document?**	Formatting symbols and hidden text
SDC PUBLICATIONS **Which tab is the header and footer tools found on?**	Page Setup
SDC PUBLICATIONS **Name the three Page Background commands found on the Design tab.**	1. Portrait 2. Landscape

SDC PUBLICATIONS **Name the command used to search for text and the Ribbon tab it is found on.**	True; Layout → Size → More Paper Sizes
SDC PUBLICATIONS **Command used to jump to another location within document.**	[vertical] Line
SDC PUBLICATIONS **What does the icon on the Home tab, with the paragraph symbol, toggle on and off?**	The entire document
SDC PUBLICATIONS **Name the dialog used to create/modify Margins.**	Insert
SDC PUBLICATIONS **What are the two orientation options for a page?**	1. Watermark 2. Page Color 3. Page Borders

SDC PUBLICATIONS **Which command can be used to create a PDF file?**	File (tab) → Info → Check for Issues
SDC PUBLICATIONS **Name the location of the document properties.**	Replace
SDC PUBLICATIONS **Name the location of the print settings.**	Insert
SDC PUBLICATIONS **True or False: The current Word document can be attached to a new email.**	Text Effects
SDC PUBLICATIONS **Name the command used to check for hidden properties or personal information.**	Format Painter

SDC PUBLICATIONS **Where can the Check Accessibility command be found?**	Save As
SDC PUBLICATIONS **Name the command used to swap one word for another.**	File (tab) → Info
SDC PUBLICATIONS **Which Ribbon tab is the Symbol command located on?**	File (tab) → Print
SDC PUBLICATIONS **Which command can make the selected text look like it has a reflection?**	True; File (tab) → Share
SDC PUBLICATIONS **Tool used to apply various settings of selected text to another selection of text.**	Inspect Document

SDC PUBLICATIONS **Which Ribbon tab is Line and Paragraph Spacing found on?**	Convert Text to Table
SDC PUBLICATIONS **True or False: Paragraph indentation can be set within the Paragraph dialog**	False; Select table, Layout (tab) → Convert to Text
SDC PUBLICATIONS **Feature used to apply standard formatting options to text.**	Insert → Table
SDC PUBLICATIONS **Location of 'Clear Formatting' command.**	Sort
SDC PUBLICATIONS **Name the type of break used to force the text to the next column.**	Layout → Cell Margins

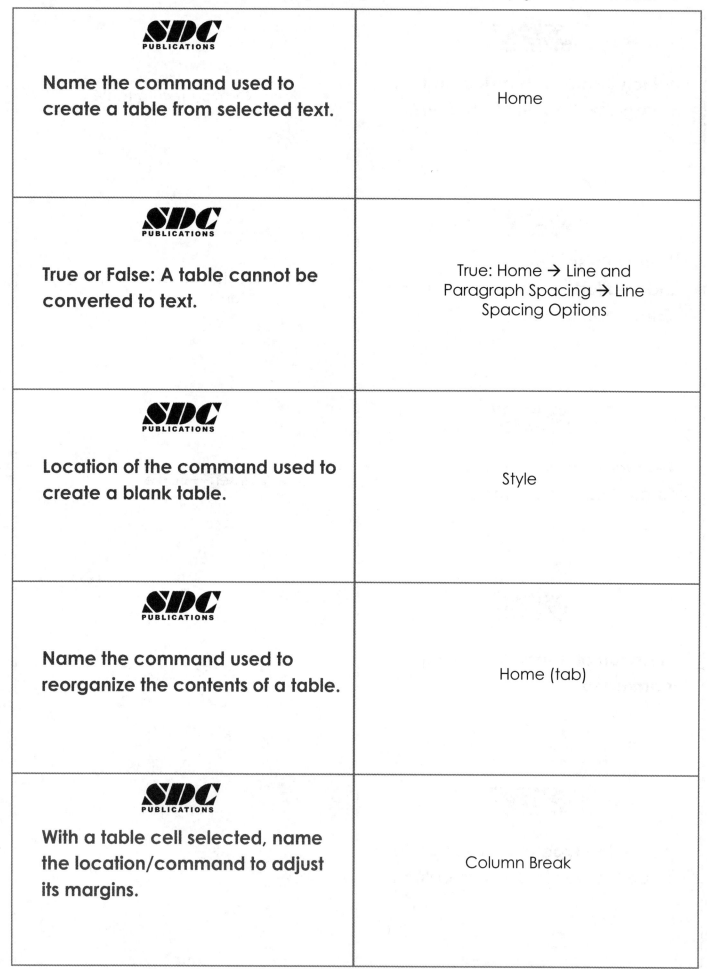

Name the command used to create a table from selected text.	Home
True or False: A table cannot be converted to text.	True: Home → Line and Paragraph Spacing → Line Spacing Options
Location of the command used to create a blank table.	Style
Name the command used to reorganize the contents of a table.	Home (tab)
With a table cell selected, name the location/command to adjust its margins.	Column Break

SDC PUBLICATIONS **Name the command and location of the command used to combine two selected cells in a table.**	True
SDC PUBLICATIONS **True or False: All Columns in a table must be the same width.**	Home
SDC PUBLICATIONS **Name the dialog used to resize the entire table.**	Right-click → Restart at 1
SDC PUBLICATIONS **Command used to break a table into two.**	True; Right-click → Reset Numbering Value
SDC PUBLICATIONS **What is the difference between a numbered and bulleted list?**	Right-click → Continue Numbering

SDC PUBLICATIONS

True or False: Custom symbols can be used in a list.

Layout → Merge Cells

SDC PUBLICATIONS

Name the Ribbon tab where the increase and decrease indent tool can be found.

False

SDC PUBLICATIONS

How is the numbering of a list restarted at number 1?

Table Properties

SDC PUBLICATIONS

True or False: A numbered list can be started at any number.

Split Table

SDC PUBLICATIONS

How is a numbered list forced to continue from a previous list?

Number/letter versus Symbol

SDC PUBLICATIONS **What is the main difference in location between footnote and endnote?**	1. PNG 2. JPG
SDC PUBLICATIONS **Name the Ribbon tab location of the footnote and endnote commands.**	Insert
SDC PUBLICATIONS **True or Fales: The Source Manager, for bibliography citations, has a special dialog box name.**	SmartArt
SDC PUBLICATIONS **Name the Ribbon tab with the tool used to insert table of contents.**	True; Insert → Screenshot
SDC PUBLICATIONS **Name the Ribbon tab for the insert shapes command.**	Text Box

SDC PUBLICATIONS **Name two popular image formats inserted with Pictures command.**	Current page versus end of document
SDC PUBLICATIONS **Name the Ribbon tab where the 3D Models command is found.**	Reference
SDC PUBLICATIONS **Which command is used to create a group of connected shapes?**	True
SDC PUBLICATIONS **True or False: A portion of the current screen can be captured and placed within the document.**	Reference
SDC PUBLICATIONS **Name the command used to place text at any location.**	Insert

SDC PUBLICATIONS **Name the command used to convert an image to make it look hand sketched.**	True
SDC PUBLICATIONS **Name the command used to make an image look like a 3D box.**	1. Drag orbit icon in view 2. 3D Model Views on Ribbon
SDC PUBLICATIONS **Name command that can format an image to have a soft oval edge.**	Simply click within it
SDC PUBLICATIONS **Name the Ribbon tab where the Remove Picture Background command can be found.**	1. Select shape 2. Right-click 3. Select Edit Text
SDC PUBLICATIONS **With an image selected, which Ribbon tab can the Width and Height parameters be found on?**	True

SDC PUBLICATIONS	
True or False: New elements can be easily added to existing SmartArt instances.	Artistic Effect
SDC PUBLICATIONS	
Once placed, 3D Models can be adjusted in which two ways?	Picture Effects
SDC PUBLICATIONS	
Add or edit text by doing what to a text box?	Picture Style
SDC PUBLICATIONS	
Name the steps required to add text to a shape.	Picture Format
SDC PUBLICATIONS	
True or False: Layout Options controls how elements interact with adjacent text.	Picture Format

SDC PUBLICATIONS **What is the purpose of Alt Text for graphic elements?**	Lock Tracking
SDC PUBLICATIONS **Which feature is used to communicate recommended changes to a document?**	50 Minutes
SDC PUBLICATIONS **True or False: Comments cannot be deleted.**	Mark for Review
SDC PUBLICATIONS **Name the feature that documents modifications made to a document.**	True
SDC PUBLICATIONS **True or False: Tracked changes can be accepted.**	False; the results are provided immediately after completing the exam.

SDC PUBLICATIONS

Name the feature that can prevent others from turning off Track Changes.

Aids people with visual impairments when using a text reader.

SDC PUBLICATIONS

How much time is allotted for the certification exam?

Comments

SDC PUBLICATIONS

During the exam, how should you mark a question if unsure of the answer?

False: Review → Delete

SDC PUBLICATIONS

True or False: You will have to use Microsoft Word during the exam.

Track Changes

SDC PUBLICATIONS

True or False: You do not find out if you passed the exam until several days later.

True